YOUR UNSEEN ENEMY
REVEALED

DR. MARIA KRINOCK

ISBN-10: 0692666427
ISBN-13: 978-0692666425

PREFACE

According by the American Foundation for Suicide Prevention, suicide is the tenth cause of death in America today. There are over 42,000 suicides every year. For every suicide that happens there are at least ten attempts of suicide. This mean there are 420,000 attempts every year. This is a lot of people who are suffering every year.

Alaska, where I invest a great deal of time ministering, has been ranked as one of the highest suicidal rates in the nation per capita. Alaska has 22 suicides per 100,000 population. There were 167 suicides alone in 2014. Thanks to prayer warriors in Alaska it has dropped from being the number one position to the number two position in the country.

People everywhere are calling suicide in America an "epidemic". I read an article in one of the California newspapers which stated in an area of one of the counties there had been a 27 percent increase in suicide. The article proceeded to say, "Local experts have no explanation for the increase." This is the case everywhere. No one really has any concrete information of why people take their own lives early.

Agencies literally spend millions of dollars for suicide prevention. I commend them for trying to solve a problem, but throwing money at it is not the answer. Until people are ready to face the truth about suicide, that there is no rational reason for one to take their own life, and that it is an outside spiritual force, then suicide rates will continue to grow higher.

Suicide has to be confronted on the spiritual level. Suicide is an outside spiritual force that plagues and harasses a person. Agencies can continue to spend millions only to see the suicide rate increase, as money will not stop a spirit from forcing its will onto people.

It is The Church that has the answers to suicide. I pray that secular agencies will not ignore the wealth that The Church (the body of

Christ) has in its arsenal. It is the body of Christ that has been given authority and power of this evil spirit. The only areas I have seen suicide stats decrease is where prayer intercessors have gathered. If agencies would turn to The Church, their efforts would be increasingly and dramatically fruitful.

In this book, you will find out why people end their life early. It has nothing to do with quality of life, or circumstances. This book will explain and show how the suicide spirit operates. I encourage any secular organization to incorporate this book into their programs and see the results for themselves.

Stats by:

American Association of Suicidology http://www.suicidology.org
American Foundation for Suicide Prevention http://afsp.org/

DEDICATION

This book is dedicated to
the Father , the Son (Jesus Christ) and the Holy Spirit.
For His purposes and His Kingdom

And...

To all the people who have partnered with us
to defeat the spirit of suicide and help us deliver this
book into the villages of Alaska!
We love you!

SPECIAL ACKNOWLEDGEMENTS

Special thanks to my loving husband who has supported me in this effort in bringing light to the villages of Alaska, and to equip the people in being set free of suicide, depression, anxiety and addiction.

****

Special thanks to my mother and father in the faith, Drs. Christian & Robin Harfouche. Without your <u>love</u>, training and equipping of the Word and Spirit of God, this book would not have been possible. I know I speak for many when I say, "I am forever grateful for your labor of love towards us disciples."

****

Special thanks to all the pastors and ministers in the villages of Alaska who serve the people of the land every day. I pray this book helps you in your endeavors in ministering to the people of God

****

A very special "thank you" to my earthly parents who raised me in Christ, and loved me no matter what and have given me their blessings on this book. I love you, Mom and Dad.

****

CONTENTS

ENDORSEMENTS

During my time in Alaska I fell in love with the Alaskan people. It's been our pleasure to return to have yearly schools of signs and wonders and, at these meetings, see many of our friends from the villages—some who come from as far as Barrow.

I have seen with my own eyes the need for help, especially to the village teenagers. Maria Krinock has earned a doctorate from The International Miracle Institute and we are honored to endorse her ministry and her work in the villages of Alaska.

God's servant,
Dr. Robin Harfouche

"This insightful and inspirational book provides a spiritual solution to the problem of suicide among the natives in Alaska and anywhere for that matter! This very personal story is a must read to anyone thinking of taking their own life. Read it: the life you save may be your own."

~Reverend William H. Nicholson
Sr. Pastor, Anchorage Moravian Church

"And you shall know the truth , And the truth shall set you free." Jesus Christ (John 8:32)

Thanks to Dr. Maria Krinock, we now have spiritual insights in how to be free from the spirit of suicide. Please read and share her story with your family and friends.

~Pastor Lowell Sage Jr
Kivalina Alaska Friends Church
Alaska Statewide Suicide Prevention Council , member

Suicide is epidemic in Alaska and leaves a wide swath of destruction in its wake. Dr Krinock's testimony and life experience recorded in this book will be a good tool in helping to correct this problem. I highly recommend anyone dealing with suicidal thoughts to read this book.

~Dick Strutz, Anchorage, Alaska

This is the story of a real life, a real battle and how to achieve and maintain the authority and power to overcome every devil! Maria has opened up her heart and most private, personal life to share with you the answer to the victory over suicide. Suicide rages in the State of Alaska as if it were some super power but Maria calls this evil spirit out and by the Word of God exposes the deceitful and defeated thing that it truly is. I have watched Maria's life for 20 years and continue to cheer at the anointed and powerful Woman of God that she has become.

~Candy Sunderland, Palmer, Alaska
Increase Alaska Ministries

Over the past 30 years of ministry I have struggled with a definitive way to help bring healing to those who struggle with suicide and the spirit of suicide. It is time to recognize what this epidemic is, call it out, cast it out and see America's young people delivered. This is absolutely the best resource on the topic I have read. I commend Maria for her honesty and believe thousands of lives will be saved through this work.

Apostle Jolynn DiGrazia
Westside Ministries, Turlock, California

Dr. Maria Krinock has written the definitive work on the subject of suicide and how to approach the treatment and permanent healing from a spiritual perspective. This work is nothing less than a textbook and should be on the desk of every professional involved with helping people. Very little has been written about this subject and certainly nothing with this degree of clarity and insight with the power to permanently deliver the suicidal individual from the spirit of suicide.

~Dr. Sammi J. Ripley
Bangor, Maine

Dr. Maria's straight talk about the reality of an enemy that is out to destroy and the powerful testimony of a God who delivers us out of this snare brings great hope, help and healing. This is a must read!

~JoAnne Meckstroth
Women of Impact Ministries

INTRODUCTION:
SUICIDAL? THERE IS HOPE!

Are you hurting today? Are you thinking about ending your life? Have you been overcome with feelings of hopelessness and despair? Do you feel trapped as if there is no way out? Do you feel like your life is out of control? Do you feel like you cannot face another day? Do you sometimes feel there is something else in the room with you, trying to push you to take your own life?

What if I told you that you have been deceived? What if I told you that you have been lied to? What if I told you that you have been conned? Would that make you mad?

What if you were in a cabin on a ship, in the middle of the ocean during a violent storm, and a crew member of the ship comes bursting through your cabin door and tells you frantically that the ship has hit a large iceberg. The crew member proceeds to tell you that the ship has been damaged and there is a hole in the ship and it is sinking fast... and what if you were told that the life raft was un-operable so there was no use in using that for your escape. What if you were told all the radio communications have been shorted out due to the storm? There is no way to contact the coast guard for help. What if you were told there is no way to get off this sinking ship... that without a shadow of a doubt the ship is going down, and there is no hope?

As you ponder that you have been told there is no hope, you feel the effects of the outside storm. You can literally feel the waves that are raging at the rate of 50 foot swells and crashing against the side and the bow of the ship. You can feel the wind that is blowing the ship in every direction. The wind is so strong that it's tearing the ship apart. It appears there is no way out. You are trapped. You are going to drown.

Then what if you were presented with another way out of the horrific death of drowning by taking some pills and falling asleep? You take the pills and fall asleep to your death, because you were told there was no way out… when you get to the "other side" you find out the truth…the ship was never sinking, there was no hole, and there was nothing wrong with the ship- you were lied to. You were conned. You find out there was a real storm, but it was temporary, and the weather settled down an hour after you took the pills. You thought what you heard and felt was the truth, yet it was not the truth. You thought what you heard, felt and saw was reality. It was not. Now you are dead. You have been deceived into taking your own life and there is no going back. My friend, this is SUICIDE.

You are the ship, and suicide wants you to think there is something wrong with you. Suicide is the work of an outside entity. Every living creature, including humans have a strong natural instinct for self preservation. Suicide is totally un-natural. Suicide is a devil that deceives and lies to you that your ship is going down, when it is not.

> **Suicide is a devil. In this book,**
> **we are going to call suicide for what it really is.**

Suicide is a devil. *(If you do not believe in demons, or the spiritual realm, I encourage you to read this book in its entirety before making that decision.)* This devil causes you to feel great emotion of being trapped, hopeless, and depressed and no way out. Yet there is nothing wrong with your ship. There is nothing wrong with you, instead it is a spirit, it is an outside force, a devil that is trying to convince you otherwise.

Many people who are dealing with suicide are feeling very overwhelmed with emotion. We treat people that are overwhelmed as if it is "natural", but yet it is not natural, it is actually a very dangerous spirit that needs to be dealt with by the Word of God.

Even the dictionary recognizes that "overwhelmed" is an outside force":

1. *To overcome completely in mind or feeling:*
2. *To overpower or overcome, especially with superior forces; destroy*
3. *To crush: to cover or bury beneath a mass of something, as floodwaters, debris, or avalanche, submerge*

When we say we are overwhelmed we are saying we have been completely overcome with great emotion, that we have been overpowered and buried by a superior outside force. This is not good! When you feel overwhelmed you feel as if something is overtaking you and you feel as if there is no control or hope. This is not normal for a human being. God did not create you or me this way. When you feel overwhelmed it is the beginning of an outside force trying to put its "feelings" on you. Overwhelmed is not something that comes from within a person, but instead from outside a person.

The bottom line is suicide is a devil. In this book we are going to call a dog a dog, a duck a duck and a devil a devil. Again, if you do not believe in demons, or the spiritual realm, I encourage you to read this book first before making that decision. I will explain what suicide is and how it operates through my personal life story and more importantly through the Word of God.

If you are hurting today, and feeling like your life is out of control, there is hope, and your storm is temporary. Don't jump off the ship! Stay onboard with us, as God by His Holy Spirit is going to minister to you through this book.

If you are dealing with suicidal thoughts of any kind you will have an opportunity at the end of this book to pray a prayer that will set you free from that devil and be introduced to Jesus.

If you are a Christian and even if you already know Jesus and you need deliverance from a suicide spirit you will also have the opportunity to receive your deliverance. I just ask that you read this book completely, and read it in faith, believing God for your deliverance, believing God that as you read this book you are receiving His grace and His power for your freedom.

CHAPTER ONE:
A GUN AT MY HEAD

Over 16 years ago, I woke up one morning in Anchorage, Alaska with an overwhelming, evil presence in the room. Although I couldn't see anyone, I could swear there was another person in the room besides myself. This presence was forcing me to pick up a gun and point it at my head. Something was over-riding my will, and making me pick up the gun. It was not me. It was as if someone was in the room with me, grabbing my body and making it do things I didn't want to do. This presence was literally pushing me to take my own life. With tears streaming down my face, and my hands trembling, it took every ounce of strength and whatever will power I could muster up to not pull the trigger.   This outside force was pushing the gun towards my head and I was trying to push the gun away. I didn't know at the time that I had an "unseen enemy".

I am a Christian woman of God. How did I get to this place? I grew up in church. I grew up in a Christian home. How can a Christian, who loves the Lord be in a place where they are about to pull the trigger?

I was privileged to grow up in a Christian home in the small town of Bothell located in the State of Washington. We were a family of five. I was the middle child, with a younger and older brother. I had a mom and a dad who loved Jesus. In today's society not many children get to grow up with two parents anymore, but instead just one, either a mom or a dad. I am ever so grateful that I had both parents who loved me, and brought me up the best they knew how. My dad worked in Seattle at Boeing and my mom worked at a tire company as a receptionist to help make ends meet. My parents understood the value of good work ethic and imparted that to us kids. My parents also believed in church life. We went to church every Sunday morning, Sunday night and mid-week on Wednesdays. Although church was not an option growing up, and there were times I resented it, I will always be grateful to my parents for bringing me up in church!

Our family unit was large and full of joy with aunts, uncles, cousins, grandpas, and grandmas. There was a lot of love and strength in our family. All the family members would get together for holidays, and at many other times throughout the year just to be together to fellowship. Our family always acknowledged Christ with prayer at every family gathering. We were a Christian family.

My earliest childhood memories are of love and joy with cousins playing together, and being loved by aunts, uncles and grandparents. I remember spending loads of time with our extended family, with good food around the table. There was nothing like Grandmas' homemade noodles! Everyone fought over the noodles! We would always meet at grandma and grandpas house for our family gatherings. The adults would play chess and card games while we kids took over grandma and grandpa's property and played cops and robbers or cowboys and Indians. In the winter, after the snow would fall, all of us kids would go sledding down grandma and grandpas steep driveway, and in the summer we had big barbeques with homemade ice cream and boating on the lake. I can still taste the homemade ice cream! Life was good.

Being we grew up in a small town, it wasn't uncommon for my brother and me to ride our bikes around town. The town was part of our playground. We would play at the Lutheran Church down the street as well as the local the post office. I remember playing with neighbor kids at the post office, sticking water balloons in the tail pipes of the mail trucks…well until we got caught by the police! Then the water balloon saga stopped after that. We made the three or four neighborhood block radius our turf when it came to playing until we would hear mom call us home for dinner. You didn't want to miss mom's fried chicken and mashed potatoes! She knew how to make a mean fried chicken meal.

THE FIRST TIME THE DEVIL THREATENED TO KILL ME

When I was seven years old I was kid-napped, and sexually abused. One day, I decided to hop on my bike and head down to the store to get an ice cream bar. It was a bright sunny day, seemed like a perfect thing to do. As I glided down the hill towards the small town grocery store, I came to one of the busier streets. My parents had taught me to get off my bike and walk it across the street. I got off my bike to get ready walk my bike across the street when a young clean cut man in a business suit approached me. He kindly asked, "Can I help you walk your bike across the street?" I thought that was awful nice of the man to offer to help me across the street, so I let him assist me to the other side of the street. When we got the other side I said, "thank you" and he replied, "you are welcomed" and I went on my way and he went on his way.

The mission was ice cream, and I must fulfill my mission, so I hopped back on my bike and continued towards the store. Once I got to the store, I parked my bike by the front entrance where all the kids parked their bikes. I had arrived at my destination and now it's time to find that perfect ice cream bar…oh yes, the chocolate cookie crust with the vanilla ice cream center. I grabbed my ice cream bar and proceeded to the checkout stand, and headed outside to eat my ice cream on that sunny day. After consuming the ice cream, the mission was completed and it was time to head back. I hopped back on my bike and began my short journey home.

As I was riding my bike through the church alley, there was that man again. The same clean cut man who had helped me cross the street earlier who seemed so nice was there. He waved to me, and I waved backed. He motioned for me to come over, so I rode my bike right up to him. I noticed he had a bike too, it was much bigger than mine. It was a ten speed. I just had a regular kid's bike. As I approached this man, he asked me, "How was the ice cream?" Of course it was delicious! He began to ask me other questions, and asked me where I lived. I was a block away from home. I was so close to home that I was able to point out the big yellow house on the corner where I lived. After I pointed out where I lived, this nice man then all of a sudden out of nowhere pulled out a big knife! It was a thick knife. It looked like one of those fishing knives with the hook on the end of it. He said that he needed me to come with him, and if I didn't do what he said, he would kill me. This was very confusing for me as a young girl. The first time I met this man he was so nice and now he has a knife and is threatening to kill me if I do not go with him. In my mind there was no option, I must go with this man or I'm going to be split into two pieces. I hopped up on the back of his bike and he began to petal. As we began to ride out of the church parking lot, I see my older brother a far off. My brother yells to me, "Where are you going with that man, Maria?" The man on the bike told me to tell my brother that he was my friend and not to worry. Already being terrified of this man from his threat to kill me, I obeyed him and I yelled back to my brother, "He is my friend, I'll be back soon."

IF YOU TELL ANYONE WHAT I DID TO YOU, I WILL KILL YOU

The man took me a few miles away from home. Further than I had ever been on my own. I wasn't exactly sure of where I even was. He took me to a dirty gas station, and escorted me into the men's room, that probably hadn't been cleaned in days or weeks. The smell of urine filled the bathroom. The man proceeds to tell me to take my pants off and lay on the dirty cement floor. I obey the man, and as I obey his commands, he has that knife in plain sight to be sure I know if I do not do what he says there will be consequences to pay. As he also proceeds to take his pants off and he puts his private parts up against me, I begin to leave my body and watch from above. He proceeded to touch me in places where a little girl should never be touched, for what seemed like an eternity at the time, and then after he was done molesting me he urinated all over me. *(It was almost as if the devil was marking his territory as if I belonged to him, like a dog marks his territory.)* I was frightened and didn't understand why this man was doing these things to me. I didn't know what shame was at that time, but I sure felt it. When he was done with his dirty business on my body, he put the knife in my face and said, "If you tell anyone what I did to you, I know where you live and I will come through your bedroom window, and **I WILL KILL YOU**." As a frightened little girl, I shook my head and acknowledged I understood what he was saying. As I gathered my clothes back on and slipped out of the men's room I now needed to find my way home. I knew the general direction of our house, and began my journey home.

When I had finally made it home, I came up to the front door and I saw my mom through the screen door. I'll never forget that memory, she was sitting on a brown leather stool waiting for me. She had her head in her hands, and I knew that she was praying. I came through the door and she lifted her head out of her hands, and with tears and fear in her face she grabbed me and hugged me and asked if I was alright. "I'm alright, mom", I said.

When my brother had seen me with that man on the bike, he had notified my parents, who had called the police. They had been looking for me all that afternoon, as I had been reported "missing". My dad, my brother and the police had a combined effort in patrolling the area looking for me while my mom stayed at home base in case I should return there. I don't know how long I was actually gone, but it was long enough.

After I had arrived home, my parents took me to the hospital to be sure I was ok **physically**, and then to the police station to file a report. Even for a seven year old girl it was hard to repeat out loud what this man had done to me. I was embarrassed and I felt shameful as if I did something wrong.

After the hospital and police visit, I was finally on my way home. It had been a long day, and I was ready to be home. As my parents tucked me in bed for the night, I remembered the words of the man, *"If you tell anyone what I did to you, I know where you live, and I will come and KILL YOU."* Oh no! I've told my parents, I've told the hospital, and now I've told the police! I immediately told my mom, "I'm scared, mom. The man said he would come kill me if I told anyone." My mom trying to comfort me the best she knew how at that time, responded, "It's alright honey, everything will be fine" and she turned off the light and shut the door and our family never talked about the incident again until about twenty years later. I had to keep this secret bottled up for decades before I could even begin the healing process.

This experience of this sexual abuse was the first spiritual open door to the demonic realm in my life of a spirit that had wanted to kill me. After this door from the sexual abuse was open, I began to experience strange spiritual things. Many times I would lay in bed and night, and a presence of fear would fill my bedroom. I would see what appeared to be dead men that would walk out of my bedroom closet and out my bedroom door to try to frighten me, and frighten me it did at the age of seven! I didn't know anything about devils, and I certainly didn't know that I had an open door to the demonic realm through this experience.

This experience also opened up a door to wrong relationships over the next many years. I would get involved in wrong relationship after wrong relationship. I would meet someone that seem perfectly normal at the time, and get involved with them only to find out later they had a spirit of perversion on them that would want to take advantage of me. I couldn't understand why I would always get entangled in these types of relationships, but it was due to that spiritual open door when I was abducted at age seven that needed to be shut. That door couldn't be shut until I addressed it in the spirit realm. Keeping secrets is not the right path to healing. Healing must happen in the spirit.

THE SECOND TIME THE DEVIL THREATENED TO KILL ME

It was another late night weekend in the early 1990's, at the bar. Nothing unusual for me at this time in my life, as I would spend many weekends at the bar, just like a lot of other people. I would work all week, and spend the weekends looking for something that would fill a void in my life. It was not unusual for my friends to have to carry me out of the bar and get me home. That was the kind of drinker I was. If I was going to drink, I was going to do it right! Rarely was I able to make it home without help after a night of drinking. Little did I know that this night was to be different than any of the other nights before it. Little did I know that on this night I would encounter a supernatural force. This night I was by myself. No friends around. I found myself in the bathroom of the bar, unable to lift myself up off the floor. I heard a voice… "Honey, are you ok?" Some lady from the bar found me there on the floor. I don't remember any words that I said back to her… but I do remember her asking, "Who can I call for you?" Somehow I managed to give her my cell phone. On the top of the list was the number of a Christian lady, named Kit, whom I had spoken with a few times in the past several months. The lady from the bar called Kit for me. In the middle of the night Kit came and picked me up and took me back to her home in Woodinville, Washington. I will always be grateful for someone showing me the love of Jesus. If she had not of picked me up that night, I would probably be dead right now. Who knows where I might have ended up?

LITTLE DID I KNOW I WOULD ENCOUNTER A SUPERNATURAL FORCE

I have no recollection that night of how Kit got me from the car to the spare bedroom in her home. Maybe her husband helped, maybe I walked… maybe I stumbled. I don't know. What I do remember is being in her home, and I had way over done it. It was obvious I drank way more than my body could handle as the room spun, and spun and I became sick beyond sick. After some time had passed, how much time I do not know. I began to cry out in pain. I could feel the alcohol rip through my internal organs. The pain was so great. It was as if I had drank so much that my organs couldn't filter the alcohol and it felt like what someone would feel if they were to pass a kidney stone. I have no other words to express what physical pain I felt that night. It literally felt like something was ripping my organs. As I painfully cried out a presence came into the room. It was a dark presence. It was heavy and thick. Although at the young age of seven I had experienced a spirit of fear, I had never experienced any sort of spiritual presence like what came into the room that night. I had never experienced the presence of the Lord, nor had I ever experienced such a presence of evil. It didn't take a genius to realize this was an evil presence that had entered the room. Whether it was the alcohol causing the

16

pain, or the evil presence, I really do not know. I tell you what I do know… as I continued to cry out in pain, an audible voice spoke out into the room. I was conscious enough to know this voice was not me. It was not a voice from within me, but a voice from the outside. The voice was not peaceful. The voice that came into this room was raspy like something you might hear on a horror movie, and the voice was filled with the presence of violence and evil. The voice proceeded to speak to me in that raspy tone, and said: *"Maria, I'm going to kill you."* After I heard these words spoken, I was literally freaked out, but I was so consumed with alcohol I couldn't move. I couldn't talk. I eventually passed out.

I DIDN'T KNOW THE DEVIL HAD A PLAN TO KILL ME

I awoke in the morning totally freaked out. I was in fear. For the first time in my life, I knew the spirit world was real, and it was no joke, yet I didn't know what to do, nor did any Christian seem to know what to do either! This second incident in my life seemed to open a door up more to this evil presence that would haunt me for years to come. I didn't know the devil had a plan to kill me. I didn't know his plan was going to be implemented through my thought life. All I knew at this point, is devils were real.

After this incident in my life, being so freaked out, and not knowing what to do, or where to turn, the only thing I could come up with was to check myself into a drug and alcohol clinic. Surely this would help and would get things on the right track. I was trying in my own efforts to solve this problem. In my mind, if I stop drinking the devil will go away. The first step is to admit you have a problem right?

NOT EVEN MICROSOFT COULD FILL THE VOID

After being released from rehab, I began applying for work, which seemed like the next logical step. It wasn't long before I had obtained a job at Microsoft. People were lined up out the door to get into Microsoft at that time. I didn't know anything about computers, but I got my foot in the door through the mailroom. I began working at the bottom of the barrel, but I knew I wouldn't be there long. Every day, I would deliver the mail to other Microsoft employees. I would see their name on the door of their office and I would speak out loud, "One day my name will be on one of those doors." I didn't know at the time I was implementing spiritual principals of speaking things into existence."

> *"…the God who gives life to the dead and calls into being what does not yet exist." Romans 4:17B Berean Literal Bible Translation*

It wasn't but a year later that my name was on one of those office doors as I had been promoted into the Windows 95 / Dos 6.0 group at Microsoft. I was no longer in the mailroom. I was now working one of the jobs people dreamed about having! I was able to set my own work schedule, no boss looking over my shoulder, and I had excellent benefits including stock options. Microsoft at that time would have amazing parties with unlimited bar, unlimited catered food and they would bring in big name bands such as "Chicago" for us. All my friends envied me working at Microsoft. During my time at Microsoft, I was able to get myself financially stable. I had my stock options, 401k plan, great house, sports car and a motorcycle– I had everything a single girl needed. I was living the American dream…. or so I thought.

While working at Microsoft something began to cry out from deep within me. Microsoft couldn't fill that empty void in me. It couldn't fill that space of unhappiness that had resided in me for so long. I considered myself a Christian. Why am I so unhappy? This unhappiness turned into depression. I excelled greatly at Microsoft as I was promoted time and time again, even so, this depression had me in a place where it took everything within me to get to the office by noon. Everything in my life felt like a thousand pounds of weight. I constantly had thoughts of "I'm not good enough". These thoughts quickly turned into more severe thoughts of "I'm not worthy of love or anything good." These thoughts turned into a force of self-hatred.

It wasn't long before that same evil presence that had spoken to me a few years earlier would appear in the room and would push me to drink to numb the pain of the feeling of unworthiness, self-hatred and depression. After months of this it wasn't just alcohol anymore, but it went to a whole different level. With the great medical benefits, I was able to go to the doctor and fake something and get free pain meds. I would fake horrible migraine headaches just to get pain medication. Now I'm not just taking alcohol to numb the pain, and to drown out the thoughts, but I'm adding narcotics to it. A rage began to build up inside me of this self-hatred and thoughts of "who could really love me?" Thoughts of "I am not lovable" and "I am unworthy of love." The greater these thoughts grew, the more drugs I used and the more I began to act out.

It wasn't long before this presence would push me to take razor blades and begin to slash my arms. It was not something I wanted to do. Something was making me cut myself. The more I cut myself, the more I hated myself. The more I hated myself, the more I cut myself and did what I could to suppress the feelings, and get to a place of numbness. It seemed like there was no end to this cycle. No end to the pain I felt on the inside. Yet there was no logical reason for this pain.

I would try to go to different churches during this time in my life. I would go hoping to find something that would fix what was inside me, not understanding that the pain, was really coming from an outside force and within. No church that I attended had any sort of life or presence of the Lord. I didn't know what I was even looking for at church. I tried almost every denomination, looking for an answer. In the natural I was living comfortably. There was no financial stress. No relationship stress. I had good friends, good job, no family pressures or issues. This simply does not make sense. Was I just having a pity party? What is wrong with me?

I'M GOING TO DIE!

After working for approximately five years at Microsoft, I awoke one morning again with that same evil presence in the room of that night I had over dosed on alcohol. As I awoke I supernaturally had a knowing. That knowing was, "I'm going to die." I know that if something does not change in my life that I'm going to die. Yet I don't know how to save myself from dying. I am powerless. I'm full of hopelessness. I tried rehab and it didn't change me. I tried church. It didn't change me. I tried both secular and Christian counseling, and nothing changed me. I tried immersing myself in seventy hour weeks on the job, that didn't fix anything. What am I missing? What is wrong with me?

Desperate times call for desperate measures. After coming to the revelation that I'm going to die, in 1996, I walked into my boss' office at Microsoft and I looked him straight in the eye and said, "I need a month off work to go to Alaska. If you do not give me a month off, then I quit." Why Alaska? I have no idea, except that it was the Lords planning and intervention for my life. I had no friends in Alaska. I had no job opportunities up there. I had no connections whatsoever. For Pete sakes, I don't even like snow! My only explanation, I realized many years later, is that it was the Lord Jesus leading me up there, in His divine plan and purpose for my life.

My boss looked shocked as I made my request for time off. His response was, "Well (with a long pause), take a month off then, I don't want to lose you, Maria. You are a good employee." "Just be sure and come back to work", he said as if he knew something I didn't know. I had every intention of coming back to Microsoft.

In June of 1996, I packed up my motorcycle in the back of my little navy blue 1989 Toyota 4x4 truck, and headed up the Alaska Highway. In my mind, I was going to "find myself" and come back a different person. I left in June of 1996 on vacation… and still today, I'm on vacation!!! I never returned to Microsoft!!!

ALASKA OR BUST!

As I drove up the Alaska Highway towards a new destination, I felt in my spirit that somehow I was stepping into destiny. In my mind, I'm on a quest! However it takes more than a destination change to change your destiny. Running from life, and running from the hopelessness, the pain, and the thoughts I struggled with were not going to go away just because I'm traveling up the Alaska Highway! Nevertheless, I felt there was something good that was about to happen in my life the closer I got to Alaska. I had no idea what awaited me when I got there, and I was not necessarily interested in meeting God, instead I was interested in "finding myself". Whatever that means!

FINDING MYSELF

When I arrived in Anchorage, Alaska… finding myself wasn't necessarily so easy. Where did I find myself? Back at the bar!!! I don't remember too much about the first few weeks in Alaska as I was loaded most of the time. Something happened after those two weeks though. Everywhere I went in the city of Anchorage, I would

21

run into a woman. It was not just "any" woman. It would always be a woman that was a Holy Spirit filled Christian who went to a church called: Anchorage Christian Center. No matter if I went to the grocery store I would run into a Holy Spirit filled Christian woman who would invite me to church at Anchorage Christian Center. If I went to the post office, I would run into a Holy Spirit filled Christian woman who would invite me to church at Anchorage Christian Center. If I went to fuel up my truck, I would run into a Holy Spirit filled woman from Anchorage Christian Center who would invite me to church! I finally gave in, and decided I would go to church! But how could this church be any different than all the rest I had gone to? I had tried several churches in my home city and none of them had any effect.

I walked into the church of Anchorage Christian Center that Sunday morning. I was fashionably late driving up on my Honda CB1 motorcycle. I was the person no one wanted to sit next to at church as I walked in wearing my black leathers, and my helmet under my arm, and my hippie, bushy hair that draped down my back. I arrived as they were in praise and worship. They were all jumping up and down in praise unto the Lord Jesus, with their hands raised and on top of that, many were dancing in the aisles! I had never seen anything like this in church growing up! Dancing in the aisles? Seriously? And they were all so happy! I was very uncomfortable in this atmosphere. It wasn't something I was used to for church. I was used to a very quiet church where maybe one or two people would raise their hands in worship. I certainly had never seen anyone dance in church before! The only thing I saw in church growing up was people crying, running to the altar. I never saw anyone overcome with joy, and I never saw anyone get a physical miracle and I certainly never saw anyone get delivered of depression. I was so uncomfortable with this atmosphere that I finally left. I left before the worship gathering was even over. I decided what I saw that morning was most certainly not of God. It was just a bunch crazy people!

THE VEIL LIFTED

The next Sunday, I decided to try church again. However, I was not going to go to that crazy church. I was going to go to one of the denominations I grew up in. As Sunday approached I got on my motorcycle and headed towards the church. I walked into this church of the same denomination I was raised in from a child, and for the first time in life, there was a veil that was lifted off my eyes. For the first time I could see. There was NO LIFE IN THIS CHURCH. I do not know how to explain it, except this church was dead. It was just a bunch of bumps sitting on logs, as if they were watching a show. There was no laughter, no joy, no dancing, no hands raised unto the Lord, no expression of life whatsoever. It was just people going through the motions. When this veil was supernaturally lifted off my eyes, I realized that crazy church must have something, these other churches did not. I needed to find out!

GOD, YOU HAVE ONE MONTH!

In my heart, I told God… "If you are really real, I give you one month to show yourself to me at that crazy church, Anchorage Christian Center." "You know the church, God the one

where all those people are jumping up and down, dancing…they seem happy."

After a month of attending Anchorage Christian Center the Lord Jesus had revealed Himself in ways that I had never experienced before, where I knew that I knew God was real and that the only way to God was through His Son Jesus. I had come to the understanding and revelation in my spirit, not just my head, that

Jesus loved me. Me! He loved me! He paid the price on the cross for my sin, and I no longer needed to punish myself with cutting my arms with razor blades or drowning my sins in alcohol and drugs. I was unhappy because I had not allowed the Lord Jesus to be my Savior and to change my nature into His nature. I had been trying to do everything myself. I was finally at the end of myself. I could not help myself out of the alcohol. I couldn't kick the narcotic drugs myself. I couldn't keep myself from cutting my arms with razor blades. I could not control my thought life that was causing these harmful things and the suicidal thoughts that were flooding my mind on a daily basis. That evil presence was trying to kill me, but once I received Jesus my whole life changed!

Now, even though my whole life changed, and I was now on the right track with the Lord, I still had issues in my soul that needed healing and deliverance. <u>We come to Christ AS WE ARE.</u> This means we don't give up the drinking, smoking, or the drugging before we come to Him. We come to Him first, and then He helps us to change from the inside out. Not from the outside in. The devil works from the outside in. Christ works from the inside out. I had come to Him, and given up on my efforts and was ready for His life changing work in my life. It was an explosion of joy, peace and love in my life like I had never experienced. For the first time in my life there were no suicidal thoughts running through my head. Just peace. There was no desire to drink or do drugs. Just peace. I was loved by God Himself. I no longer needed to punish myself. He paid price for me.

Although I immediately quit drinking and I quit using drugs, there was still something there lurking behind the scenes…waiting to make its move. Months had gone by since I had received Jesus as my Lord and Savior. I was enjoying life, enjoying the love of God, enjoying my new spiritual family at church. However, there would be times when out of nowhere, I would be driving down the road and a presence would fill the truck. That same evil presence that came to me when I had over dosed on alcohol and audibly spoke to me. This presence would at times come to me and fill up the room with its evil and try to get me to drink and cut myself again. The presence was so overwhelming at times, that once in a while I gave in to it... and I would later have to repent and ask the Lord to forgive me. Even after giving my life to the Lord, that evil presence would occasionally (not often) come back to haunt me, and taunt me especially in my thought life. There would be times of such hopelessness, despair and depression that would hang over me like a dark cloud, all I could do was curl up in a ball on my bed and cry.

Even though I was so happy to be a new creation in God, so happy to be in relationship with the Holy Spirit, I kept my battles to myself. I didn't tell anyone that every now and then this evil would fill my room, and try to get me to use drugs, and flood me with thoughts of unworthiness and even suicidal thoughts. It was not there every day like it was before I received Jesus. It was like that spirit knew its days were numbered and it would just come back to haunt me every now and then. But even every now and then is too much!

REVIVAL!

I heard about a revival meeting going on down in Homer, Alaska. I decided to make the four hour trip down from Anchorage. It was a weeklong revival with two evangelists from Tampa, Florida area. I can't remember their names, but they were full of the Word and Spirit. It was about the third night of the revival. The anointing was very strong. There is something about the anointing that will agitate you when you need deliverance. I was fidgety in my seat that night. I could not sit still in this meeting. I didn't understand why. The meeting seemed like an eternity! I could not wait to get out of there. I kept looking at my watch. Finally when it was over, I shot out the door as quickly as I could. I got in my truck and was beginning to drive back to where I was staying that night at a friend's house. When I pulled up to the stop sign just outside the church parking lot, there came that haunting, evil presence again.

This time it was stronger than ever! Its presence was so thick, I could tangibly feel it. It filled my whole truck cab. It was overwhelming to say the least. The evil presence spoke to me again audibly, and it said with its raspy voice and with a forceful command, "Turn left, (instead of right, as right was to take me home to my friend's house) and go down to the bar and drink yourself to death." Tears began to pour down my face as I turned left instead of right. This presence was again, pushing me and forcing me to do something I didn't want to. I didn't want to go left and go down to the bar. I didn't want to drink myself to death. I didn't want to die. I wanted to live!

I wanted to go right at the stop sign and go back to my friend's house where I was staying. The evil presence was so strong it made me turn left to head down towards the bar. Somehow, some way by the grace of God I passed the bar instead of turning into it, and somehow by the grace of God I made it my friend's house that night. I couldn't tell you how I got there, as I have no recollection. With tears streaming down my face, I quietly got myself into bed for the night. Why am I being haunted by this presence? Why is it trying to kill me?

The next day, my friend and I headed to the fourth night of the revival. I was wondering if I could stay in my seat, because the night before I was so fidgety. At the end of the meeting that night, the Lord had shown my friend that I needed deliverance. So, she gently grabbed my hand and led me up to the front where the two evangelists were. My friend told the evangelists I needed deliverance and asked if they would pray for me. The evangelists picked up some oil they had, and they put just a drop of oil on their finger. Then they put that one finger on my forehead, and all of a sudden it felt like someone had taken a piece of flat iron metal, that had just been pulled out of the fire, and then wrapped it around my forehead! As this heat penetrated my body, my soul and my spirit all at once, I fell out under the power of the Holy Spirit. In one moment, the Anointing, the presence of the Lord, had set me free of that depression, and that suicide devil! That thing was gone! Glory to God! I was set free! The devil had been cast out of my life.

I had been burdened with that haunting, suicide, flesh cutting, addiction, depression, devil for years! In just one moment of the anointing, in just one moment of the presence of the Lord, that burden was destroyed.

> *"And it shall come to pass in that day, that his burden shall be taken away from off thy shoulder, and his yoke from off thy neck, and they yoke shall be destroyed because of the anointing."*
> *Isaiah 10:27 KJV*

This was the first major deliverance in my life from that suicide and addiction demon. It was after that deliverance that I began traveling the villages of Alaska with a team from the church helping to assist in whatever way I could in preaching the gospel. Whether it was carrying the luggage of the team, cooking for the team, doing office work for the ministry, doing laundry for the team, whatever I could find to do, I did it unto the Lord.

THE SECOND DELIVERANCE

Years had gone by, with no haunting from that suicide-addiction devil because I had been set free and delivered. I had totally immersed myself in the things of God. I was going after souls for the Kingdom of God assisting another ministry. In that time we saw many come to the Lord, and many touched by His presence. It was a good ministry. We saw salvations, healings and deliverances. However, in the midst of all that, the devil got in there and brought in a great wounding for me with that particular ministry. It was a wound that went in very deep, and I was unable to recover from it. I had pastors calling me over the phone from across the country, and asking, "Are you alright?" and they proceeded to say that the Lord had been giving them dreams that I was being raped and beaten, and they wanted to be sure I was safe. Well I wasn't being raped in the physical sense, but I was being raped in the spiritual sense. Everything was being stripped from me. I was devastated. I was crushed. It is not important to know what was done to me that wounded me so badly, but I think you get the idea, it was a bad situation!

It was through this wounding that the enemy was able to get back in my life with the spirit of suicide. This time it wasn't just a cutting of my flesh, or an over-dose of alcohol, it was full on gun pointed at my head. I was full of vivid visions of myself blowing my head off. Here I am, I have been a team member in ministering the Gospel of Jesus Christ, filled with the Spirit of God, and a gun is pointed at my head.

The Word of God says,

> *"And when he (the devil) comes, he finds it swept and put in order. Then he goes and takes with him seven other spirits more wicked than himself and they enter and dwell there; and the last state of that man is worse than the first."*
> *Luke 11:25-26 NKJV*

I now found myself in a worse state than I had been years ago. Yes, unbelievably it was actually worse than before. I was tortured in my mind by visions of killing myself, I was tortured in my mind by thoughts that were coming at me ten times greater than ever before. The thoughts were non-stop. It was literally torture. I was unable to sleep at night. Due to this wounding and un-forgiveness in my heart I had been handed over to the torturers.

> *"Then summoning him, his lord said to him, You wicked servant, I forgave you all that debt because you pleaded with me. 'Should you not also have had mercy on your fellow servant, in the same way that I had mercy on you?' And his lord, moved with anger, handed him over to the torturers until he should repay all that was owed him. My heavenly Father will also do the same to you, if each of you does not forgive his brother from your heart.*
> *Matthew 18:32-35 New American Standard Bible*

These thoughts seemed like my thoughts, but they were not. The Lord had made me a new creation. I belonged to the Lord. This was an outside force that once again was trying to overcome my will and overtake me. The devils plan had not changed for my life, his plan was still to kill me. God had a different plan, but in the meantime I was being tortured in my thought life, where the devil was trying to take my sanity.

One morning when I awoke and that evil presence was in my bedroom again. Tears flowing down my face as I held the .380 gun to my head. This thing was trying to overcome me and it was winning. I didn't want to pull the trigger. **My hands were trembling, using every bit of strength I had to not pull the trigger**. By the grace of God, I managed to escape that death and was able to put the gun down. I was in a position again, of not knowing what to do or how to get my deliverance. I cried out to God. Nothing. I heard nothing back. Why am I not hearing anything? I picked up the phone and called the ministry of where I was wounded so badly, and asked if that person would meet me for coffee. We sat there at the coffee shop in Anchorage. I'm staring the person in the eye who so badly wounded me.

As our conversation proceeded, my eyes were opened. This person had no idea that they had harmed me, or that they had wounded me, and nor that they even did anything wrong! How could that be? How could they not know that what they did was wrong? I realized they would never come to the understanding of what they did was wrong and hurtful, and I would be waiting for an apology for the rest of my life! *(Their perception of the events that happened may be totally different than mine)* I realized it is not worth it to be hurt and wounded, no matter how devastating their actions were towards me. It was not worth the pain and agony. *(What I didn't realize at the time, that by me holding on to a grudge and un-forgiveness I was just as guilty. As the Lord refers to one who does not forgive as "wicked" according to Matthew 18:32.)*

Once I reached this revelation within our coffee shop conversation that I would never receive an apology for the hurt done, the love of God supernaturally began to fill me and I reached out and grabbed this person's hand, and I looked them in the eye, and I said with all of my heart, "Please forgive me for anything I did to hurt you." As soon as I said that, that person broke into tears, and I broke into tears, and more importantly, the door to un-forgiveness was shut and I have NEVER seen that suicide, addiction, depression devil again!!!   Forgiving that person, set me free and caused all that torment and torture to leave.

Forgiveness was the key in my second deliverance.   I have been free ever since. You too can be free when you truly forgive from your heart. This is what separates the idea that suicide is in you and clarifies that suicide is an outside force, it is a spirit or as the bible calls them, a devil. If it were you, then all the despair, depression, hopelessness and suicidal thoughts would stay with you after you forgave, because you are still you!

Deliverance means to be "saved from your enemies." Deliverance will separate you from your unseen enemy. Deliverance and the power of forgiveness or the anointing of the Holy Spirit will remove that suicide devil, and you will no longer have suicidal thoughts, depression, anxiety or hopelessness. Instead you will be full of God's love, peace, joy and happiness.

In the next few chapters we will teach and expose the outside force that causes suicide, addiction and depression and how to overcome it.

CHAPTER TWO
GOD'S MASTERPIECE

There is a real spiritual war over YOU! You are prime property of God Almighty, and the devil would love to destroy what God has created so wonderfully.

> *"For we are Gods masterpiece. He has created us anew in Christ Jesus, so we can do the good things He planned for us long ago." Ephesians 2:10 NLT Trans."*

First let's get this straight, YOU are God's MASTERPIECE. Think about that for a moment. By dictionary definition, masterpiece means: *a person's greatest piece of work.*   **YOU, are God's greatest creation!!!** You are greater than anything on earth or heaven that God has created. You are greater than the trees and rivers He created and greater than the stars in the heavens. You are greater than any animal or any angelic being that God created with His own hands.   *YOU ARE HIS MASTERPIECE.* Out of everything in heaven and earth that God has created, YOU are His best work! " He created you wonderfully so that you can fulfill your destiny in Him and He has good things planned for YOUR life and future. It is not God's will for any to perish, but instead to have everlasting life for all of eternity: a forever that is filled to overflowing with His love, peace, joy and abundance. Eternity is now. It is not something far off. God has an absolutely beautiful life for you right now!

> *"For I know the plans I have for you," declares the Lord, "plans to prosper you and not to harm you, plans to give you a hope and a future." Jeremiah 29:11 NIV*

God has a plan for your life! It's not a plan to harm or hurt you. He didn't say, "I have a plan for you to end your life early"! It is not a plan of suicide nor is it a plan for you to be enslaved to addiction, depression or suicidal thoughts. His plan isn't one of poverty, but instead it is one of harvest and prosperity. God's plan begins here and now and reaches into your future. With you in mind, God has already planned, designed your life with victory and success. This plan of God is waiting for you to step into it and claim it as your own. The Word of God says, that Jesus is the *"author and finisher" of our faith. (Hebrews 12:2)* There is a book in heaven with YOUR name in it, and Jesus is the author. He has written out your victory, and finished it when He died on the cross and rose again to life. The only person that has the power to change your heavenly book is YOU! The Word of God says, that we have the power to choose life or death: ***"... I have set before you life and death, blessings and curses. Now choose life, so that you and your children may live." Deuteronomy 30:19 NIV***

I am confident that if you are reading this book, that you have already decided to "choose life". This is the beginning of a new journey in God for you. Today is a new day of this new life for you: a day of victory. Today you have dominion over your enemy. God has wonderfully made you. You are His greatest work, and He has plans of hope and a wonderful future for you!

Begin to say out loud….

- **"I AM GOD'S MASTERPIECE."**
- **"I AM WONDERFULLY MADE BY GOD."**
- **"GOD HAS A GOOD FUTRE FOR ME."**

Say these phrases out loud every day! Put them on your mirror, put them wherever you can see them. Say them out loud and speak them into being, just like I did when I claimed my Microsoft office. Listen for God. He may inspire you with other good 'identity statements' for you to say out loud every day. If He does, add those to this list! *(Romans 4:17)*

Think about it. You are such a masterpiece of God that God chose to send His ONLY son, Jesus to die on the cross for you. Since the fall of Adam, everyone is born with a sinful nature. In ourselves we can't live up to His ways. The Bible says, "all have fallen short of the glory of God", and that we need a Savior. *(Romans 3:23 KJV)* There had to be a sacrifice for sin, and God chose His Son to pay that price for YOU and for me! That is how much God loves you, and wants to have relationship with YOU. He loves you so much that He doesn't want you to have to die, but instead His Son Jesus was sent to die in your place for your sin and my sin!

He does not want you to die! It is a lie of the devil that the only way out is to end your life. It is a lie of the devil that you have to punish yourself. We all deserved punishment, but Jesus paid the punishment for us, so we do not have to. He doesn't want you to *take your own life*, instead He has a life for you that He wants to *GIVE YOU*. The Bible also says, *that "ALL who call on the name of the Lord Jesus Christ will be saved." (Romans 10:13 KJV)*

If you have not received Jesus Christ as your personal Lord and Savior, there is no need to wait till the end of this book! Salvation is a free gift. You can be saved right now! When you give your life to Jesus, then He will give you HIS LIFE. You exchange your life of despair, hopelessness, depression, addiction, sickness, poverty, and suicide for His life of peace, joy, prosperity, healing and abundance.

Just pray this prayer out loud, and mean it in your heart:

"Father God, according to your word in Romans 10:13, all who call upon the name of Jesus will be saved, and therefore I believe Your Word and I call upon the name of Jesus to save me! I ask you Lord to forgive me of all my sin, and ask you to wash me clean with your Word. I acknowledge that You sent Your only Son, Jesus for me, to pay the price for my punishment. I acknowledge that Jesus is alive today, as He rose from the dead after dying on the cross for me. Thank you God, that I am NOW SAVED, and I ask you to fill me with your free gift of the of the Holy Spirit, as it says in "Acts 2:38". I receive all healing, all deliverance, all abundance that heaven has for me now. I receive the breath of God and the life that Jesus has for me. Thank you that I am now the righteousness of Christ Jesus, and I am no longer a sinner. I am now a saint saved by faith, through the grace of God."

Welcome my friend! Welcome to your new life in Christ Jesus! Salvation is a free gift!

CHAPTER THREE:
ARE DEVILS REAL?

In the next few chapters I want to take the time to address who our enemy is so we know what we are really dealing with. If we do not know who our enemy is, then it's going to be very difficult to walk in victory. The Bible itself says,

> *"Be alert and of sober mind. Your enemy the devil prowls around like a roaring lion looking for someone to devour."*
> *1 Peter 5:8 NIV*

How is it that people say there is no devil, when this verse from the Bible clearly states we have an enemy, and that enemy is the devil? Can it get much clearer than that? What is a devil?

The best way I can think of describing a devil is a dis-embodied personality or person that is not redeemed by the Lord Jesus Christ. They are personalities with real emotions and thoughts but without a body. They are looking for physical, earthly bodies that they can utilize for their purposes.

The Bible is clearly telling us that there is a devil that is seeking out a victim, and that our mind is important when it comes in dealing with the devil. His main strategy is power of suggestion to a person, therefore *be sober minded...* in other words our mind plays a key role in how we fight the good fight of faith. The Bible is telling us to be sober minded, because our mind is what the devil is after.

How many times have you heard in the news and media of people losing their mind and doing something crazy? How many times have you heard in your own area of people losing their mind and killing their family or a shootout happening in a hospital or school? These are not normal acts. These are acts of people who are not in their right mind. If the devil can get control of your mind, then he will have control of your will. What is a sober mind? A sober mind is a mind that is set on the Word of God. A sober mind is a mind that makes the Word of God the final word in their life, and rejecting all thoughts and words that do not line up to Gods word. *"For God has not given us a spirit of fear, but of power, love and a SOUND MIND." (2nd Timothy 1:7)* God's will for us is a sober and sound mind that is fixed on Him.

It is of the utmost importance to understand that suicide symptoms and thoughts are not coming from you, but instead coming from an outside spiritual force. The devil is going after your SOUND MIND which is in your soul.

BODY, SOUL & SPIRIT

You are a human being that has three parts: you are spirit, you are soul and you are body. You are spirit, which has a soul, which lives in a body. Your soul is your mind, will and emotions. Our soul is given to us by God. However our soul when it is not born again, is under a sin nature. When it is born again, then our soul is tied into God. Even though our soul is tied into God, it is still needs to be changed and transformed by His Spirit. The more we let the Holy Spirit into our soul, into our emotions, and into our will the more we become like Christ.

The devil goes first after the mind, if we do not have a sound mind, then our will cannot make rational decisions. Our will is what the devil wants to overcome, because that is where our ability is to

38

make decisions. When a person yields their will over and over again to the lies of the devil, that will is over taken by that evil spirit. Then it will use that person's will against them, leading them to take their own life.

SIMPLE THINGS WE NEED TO UNDERSTAND:

1. The Spirit realm is real.

2. Our soul is what is being changed and transformed by His Spirit.

3. There is a heaven and there is a hell.

4. There are angels and there are devils or demons.

5. There is a God and there is a devil – satan

6. God is good and the devil is bad.

7. God desires to give you a good life, the devil desires to take your life.

Although this is simple Bible belief, not everyone believes the Bible. I grew up in church all my life. I believed in God, and His only Son Jesus, yet never believed in devils because no one ever taught about devils. How can you overcome your enemy if you don't know you have an enemy?

This is the devils greatest strategy today. To make people think he doesn't exist, so he can go around and cause havoc in people's lives and they do not know how to overcome it, because they do not know what the source of the problem is. How can you fight a problem when you have no idea where it came from? As the devil stays hidden, then people do things like medicate the problem instead of going after the spiritual side of things. Get this straight today: you cannot medicate suicide, it will delay it for a while, but it is a temporary solution. The power of the blood of Jesus is the only true answer. Prozac is not the answer. You cannot medicate a devil, nor can you counsel a devil.

Devils have to be cast out. This is not something weird or spooky as we see in the movies. It is simply commanding an outside entity (a devil) to be removed as we have been given that authority and right by Jesus. Both suicide and addiction have to be dealt with in the spiritual realm. It took an audible voice for me to even begin to realize that devils were real. When the devil out loud said to me, "I'm going to kill you." It didn't take a genius to realize that this was no joke and that devils do exist.

Let's see what the Bible has to say about devils:

The Bible tells us that there are devils and they are very real. Jesus' ministry was healing the sick and casting devils out. Many times the sickness or disease was tied to a devil and when Jesus cast the devil out, the disease left. It is the same with suicide or addiction, when you cast the suicide and/or addiction devil out, the symptoms leave with them.

So let's look at it again.

> *"When the evening was come, they brought unto Him many that were possessed <u>with devils</u>: and He <u>cast out the spirits</u> with His word, and healed all that were sick." Matthew 8:16 KJV*

What are devils? According to the Matthew 8:16, devils are spirits. Spirits are invisible. Your enemy is invisible, but that doesn't change the fact that he is there and very real. It is a fact that we breathe air. Just because we can't see the air doesn't mean it's not there. You can be sure that if you jump off a 50 foot high building that you are going to fall to the ground, due to the law of gravity. You cannot see gravity, but you do not doubt it that it's there. The word of God says in the above verse that Jesus cast out devils that oppressed the people. The Word of God also says in Mark 16:17 *"These miraculous signs will accompany those who believe: They will cast out demons in my name..."* (New Living Translation) This verse is not something of the past, but of the "now". This verse isn't even an option for a Believer, but instead it is instructions for everyone who is and is to come to Believe on the name of Jesus as a born again Believer. If God left us instructions to cast out devils, and God is not a man and that He should lie, *(Numbers 23:19)* then you can be sure devils are real even though you cannot see them.

It wasn't uncommon for Jesus to be casting out devils everywhere He went. Very often, wherever you saw His miracle working power you see devils being cast out. When the devil is cast out, symptoms leave you. When the devil is cast out, ailments leave you, whether they are physical, mental or spiritual symptoms. The root of diseases and mental illnesses is due to the effects of sin that entered the earth when mankind opened that door to satan. Sin is in direct connection with devils. If the medical community wants to call suicide and addiction a disease, then fine, the root of that disease is a DEVIL!

It's also just as important, actually it's MORE important to realize that although God is invisible to us, that HE IS ALWAYS THERE! To remember that God's word says that He will NEVER leave us or forsake us. *(Hebrews 13:5)*

Although we will be talking about devils throughout this book, to remember that God is always *GREATER* than our enemy.

That enemy has already been defeated at the cross and stripped of all his power and authority.

When you are a born again Believer, and you have become a disciple of Jesus Christ, you have The Greater one living in you.

"YOU, dear children, are from God and have overcome them, because the one who is in you is greater than the one who is in the world."
1 John 4:4

You have God Almighty living in you. If you are not a Believer, and if you have not given your life over to the Lord Jesus Christ, then you will have an opportunity to receive Christ at the end of this book, so that you too can have the Greatest Spirit in the Universe living in you!!!

> **"When the evening was come, they brought unto him many that were <u>possessed</u> with devils:.."**

The word in the above verse "possessed" really is not a good translation of this verse. The Greek word is: daimoizomai or "demonized", which means to be under the power of a demon. Possessed is not a good English word because it implies "ownership of". If you are a born again Believer and you are dealing with a spirit of any kind, you are not under the ownership of the devil as you have already been bought with a price. Jesus paid the price for you on that cross, and you belong to Him. God owns you! You are God's property!

You are wonderfully made and you are God's masterpiece.

SAY IT OUT LOUD:

"I AM GOD'S MASTERPIECE!"

"I AM GOD'S BEST WORK!"

Deliverance in Jesus' ministry was most likely an everyday thing! It wasn't uncommon for Him to be delivering people of devils, and most of them were in the synagogue, or in the church. Unfortunately many churches today, do not teach or practice deliverance, even though people need it so badly.   Jesus was ministering to the Jews: the people of God who needed deliverance. Hear me now, God's people needed deliverance! It's nothing to be ashamed of if you need deliverance. Let's not park there but step up and receive what the Lord has for us in freedom from bondage! Let's take a look at the account of a daughter who was severely demon possessed in Matthew 15:

> *Vs 22-23 And behold, a woman of Canaan came from that region and cried out to Him, saying "Have mercy on me, O Lord, Son of David!   My daughter is <u>severely demon-possessed."</u> But He answered her not a word. And His disciples came and urged Him saying, "Send her away, for she cries out after us."*

> *Vs 24-25 – But He answered and said, "I was not sent except to the lost sheep of the*

house of Israel." Then she came and worshiped Him, saying, "Lord, help me!"

Vs 26-27 But He answered and said, "It is not good to take the children's bread and throw it to the little dogs." And she said, "Yes, Lord, yet even the little dogs eat the crumbs which fall from their masters' table."

Vs 28 Then Jesus answered and said to her, "O woman, great is your faith! Let it be to you as you desire." And her daughter was healed from that very hour. (NKJV)

This woman came to Jesus with a devil problem. She is a preview of salvation and deliverance on credit for all humankind. Jesus was there for Jews at that particular time, but we know that later on the gentiles were grafted in, and received into His Kingdom. This woman pressed in for what didn't belong to her. Jesus clearly states to this woman that deliverance from devils is classified as the "children's bread". In other words deliverance is ONLY for the children of God.

The Jews at that time were the children of God, but now that we also are born of God, which makes us children of God, therefore we too are qualified for deliverance. This woman pressed Jesus for a miracle for her daughter. Jesus answered her not a word back, and she came back and put a demand on the power that Jesus was carrying. She was "going after" her deliverance. She was desperate. God responds to people who "go after" the anointing. The Bible says that those who are hungry and thirsty for righteousness shall be filled *(Matthew 5:6)*. She knew within herself with just one Word from the Messiah that her daughter would be delivered of those devils. All she had to do was receive it by faith and her severely demon possessed daughter would be healed that very hour. She didn't have to do any sort of works to earn this deliverance. We do not deserve anything that Christ has done for us. None of us have earned Gods goodness in our lives. Instead it is a free gift. Deliverance is free. You will never qualify on your own for it. You just receive what the Lord has done for you on the cross. You just yield to the power of His Spirit. This is what happened to me, when the evangelist laid hands on me for deliverance, I yielded my spirit to the Holy Spirit, and the anointing destroyed the bondage I was in. When the devil left me, all his lying thoughts of suicide and low self-esteem went with him.

Deliverance is part of our benefits of what Jesus paid for on the cross. It is the children's bread! We can partake of it because we are a child of God! If we have a problem with a devil then by all means, let's get delivered. Let's not be ashamed, but instead receive what Christ has freely given us. There are many, many Christians out there who need deliverance from suicide, depression, addiction, anxiety and from diseases and all kinds of works of the devil. If you are a Christian struggling with suicide, rejoice because you are about to get delivered and partake of the children's bread!

The battle of suicide cannot be won without the help of the Son of God, Jesus. If you think you can win this battle without the help of His Spirit, you are sorely mistaken. I tried all my own efforts for years, and it nearly killed me. I tried counseling, that didn't work. I tried medicating it with Prozac, that didn't work. I tried drowning it in alcohol and that didn't work! It was ONLY with the help of the power of the Holy Spirit that I was set free.

CHAPTER FOUR
WHAT IS SUICIDE?

This brings us back to the question, what is suicide? The dictionary will tell you that suicide is "*the intentional taking of one's own life.*" This is not completely true. The dictionary definition is implying a person makes a choice to take their own life. If this were completely true, the suicide rate would be close to zero percent as no one takes their own life in their right mind intentionally". The key word here is: "*right mind".*

Suicide is a spirit (devil) that goes after the mind and will of a person to overtake it. It pushes its mind and will onto a person. Once the mind and will is overtaken, then that spirit uses its own will to take that person's life by using the will of the person. Pushiness is not of God. The Spirit of God is a gentlemen. He doesn't force anything on His children. From the beginning God gave mankind choice. They had a choice to eat or not eat of the forbidden tree in the garden.

In the Bible there are several accounts where the devil pushes people or pressures them, bending them to his will. The boy that was thrown into the fire over and over. The boy wasn't throwing himself in the fire, a devil would do that to him. That is a forceful act. The devil when he tempted Jesus, was trying to push and pressure our Lord into worshiping him, and try to cause him to fall into sin. *(The devil was unsuccessful with Jesus, as Jesus didn't give into the devils tactics)* The demoniac in the cave with legion.

47

Those devils pushed that man to the point of insanity in his mind that he had to live in a cave as the devil had taken over his mind. Then once Jesus cast those devils out of the man, they went into the pigs and those devils drove the pigs over the cliff to kill themselves. The devil drives, pushes and forces where he can. Pressure and pushiness is never from God. He is a giver of life. He won't force you to be healed, you receive His healing. He doesn't push deliverance on you, you receive His deliverance.

The greatest thing about humankind is his or her will. God gave each person a will. It is what makes us different from all creation. Our will is our decision making faculty. Our will is where we make our decisions, good or bad. God has given us the power of choice, and He is so sovereign that He has chosen to let us make our own choices and He will not interfere with our choice. This is why we must choose God's will for our life. The devil on the other hand will do everything he can to interfere with our will and try to take possession of our will because with our will comes power of choice.

THE WILL OF MAN, AND THE WILL OF GOD

Our will is one of the most powerful things God has given us. With our will we choose our destiny. With mans will inventions are made. With mans will humanitarian works are done. With mans will wars erupt. With mans will cities and nations are built.

God also has a will. He made us in His image, and He too has a will. His will is His decision making faculty also. He has already made His decision about you. He has already decided you are His masterpiece and wonderfully made.

He has already decided that you are healed by the power of His Son Jesus, who died on the cross for you. *"By His stripes you were healed." (1ˢᵗ Peter 2:24)* He has already made up his mind for you to have an abundant and prosperous life as Jesus said, *"I have come that they might have life and life more abundantly."* (John 10:10b)

Jesus said pray this way...
"Thy Kingdom come, thy <u>WILL</u> be done
on earth as it is in heaven."
Matthew 6:10 NKJV

Gods will, His decision making faculty, has already been decided. Jesus said pray this way, because God has made up His mind about you in Heaven, and it's up to you to decide with your will that His will is a done in your life on this earth! His will is the best you can experience in life. His will is full of life, destiny, purpose, healing, deliverance and freedom. You have to line up your will, your choice with His choice for your life. When your will meets heaven will, then there is an explosion of the performance of Heaven that happens in your life. Or you can say it like this, when your decision lines up with heavens decision about you, there is a miracle!

There may be people who sacrifice their life as martyrs for Jesus, or you may find a soldier who sacrifices their life for their countrymen in their right mind. In everyday life, no one just wakes up and decides with their will, "Hey, I think I will end my life today". *There is a process, a pressure and a pushiness from an outside spirit that has led up to that point, that has caused a persons will to be weakened.* Suicide is really a slow murder. Although when it happens it is "sudden" to the rest of us, but to the person who endured, it was a slow process.

There is generally years of contemplation and spiritual torture behind the act of a suicide. This is why it is *important* to get a hold of what God has for you today, and not put it off till tomorrow. You have a destiny NOW! Suicides plan is to kill your purpose and destiny that God has ordained for you since before you were even born.

> **Even before he made the world, God loved us**
> **and chose us in Christ to be holy and without**
> **fault in his eyes. Ephesians 1:4 (NLT)**

Suicide is a spirit that you cannot see with your eyes. *Suicide is your unseen enemy*. Suicide's mission is to kill you by getting you to take your own life. There is another spiritual party involved in suicide. It is not just a person deciding to take their life, but an outside force that overcomes their will.

> "The thief comes ONLY to steal and KILL and destroy;
> I have come that they may have life,
> and have it to the full.
> John 10:10 NIV

Let's get something straight. You do have an enemy that wants to kill you, however, let's get something else straight, **YOUR ENEMY CAN'T KILL YOU!** Why? The enemy can only work in your life as much as YOU allow him to with your will. He can only work with what you give him. When I was under a spirit of suicide it was over powering my will. However, I didn't get there "overnight". It was a process of continually allowing the enemy to put thoughts and feelings in my mind and heart that were not the truth. When I had given into that spirit enough, then it tried to make me do something I didn't want to do. It was making me feel things I didn't want to feel. It was making me think things I didn't want to think. Those thoughts and feelings were so real to me, that I thought they were me and I thought they were true. They were not me. It was a devil lying to me and putting those thoughts and feelings on me (not in me) from the outside. They were a lie.

If those thoughts and feelings were me, then they would still be with me today, but the anointing of the Holy Spirit cast that devil out. When that devil left, all the thoughts and feelings left.

SAY OUT LOUD NOW:

"THE DEVIL CANNOT HAVE MY LIFE, I BELONG TO GOD."

"I AM GOD'S MASTERPIECE.THE DEVIL CANNOT KILL ME, BECAUSE HE CANNOT HAVE MY MIND AND WILL."

"I WILL TRUST IN THE LORD WITH ALL MY HEART, ALL MY MIND, ALL MY SOUL."

Ok, not all of you are saying the above out loud! You need to hear these confessions with your own ears! Say it!

The Word of God says…

> *"Give <u>NO</u> place to the devil.*
> *Ephesians 4:27 NKJV*

This means that you and I <u>CAN</u> give the devil a place in our lives. I assure you, whatever a person will give the devil, he will not be shy about taking it! I got to the point of suicide because there was no resistance to the thoughts and feelings that the enemy was putting on me, and I had no understanding of who I was in Christ. If I had resisted those thoughts, I would have never come to the place where I was holding a gun to my head!

You hear of cases all the time of people in prison, and when they are asked, "why did you commit that crime?" More often than not their answer is, "I don't know. I didn't want to do it, something made me do it." These people had surrendered their will, unknowingly, to a devil and that devil's will then took over their will. *(Again, your will is your decision making faculty.)* They allowed the devil to work through them and use their will. The devil can't force himself on a strong Christian, and he has no rights over a Christian. The only right a devil can have over a Christian is when a Christian gives him the permission to their life by yielding to that spirit. When you yield to another vehicle or pedestrian you give them the "right of way" or they get to "go first" and lead the way. This is what it means when you yield your life to the devil. You give him the right of way. This is why the Bible says to "*give no place to the devil.*" The thing about the spirit realm is you cannot see it! The devil wants to stay out of the light, and stay hidden, so that he is not identified. The devil wants you to think it's all you, and that there is something wrong with you. As soon as the light comes on him, and he is exposed, then it's over! It is not you!

Once you know that you are dealing with an invisible force and understand how he operates, then you will learn to not yield your will to him, and he will not be able to operate anymore in your life! This is something that every Believer has to develop. To develop their will in God's will so strongly that anything that opposes God's will in their life is rejected. As we learn this, instead of yielding to the devil, we will begin to yield to God's will and let Him have the right of way in our life, and let Him lead the way for us.

We do not have to be in fear that something is going to "overtake" us. Jesus has provided our way out of this mess! Just keep reading through this entire book, and be ready to receive what God has for you! Remember God is greater than any suicide devil and He is bigger than any situation. If you are reading this book you are on the right track today. We are going to show you how to give your life over to the Holy Spirit, who changes and transforms us into the image of Christ.

CHAPTER FIVE
THE GREAT LIE EXPOSED

"The thief's purpose is to steal and kill and destroy.
My purpose is to give them a rich and satisfying life.
John 10:10 NLT

Jesus has come with purpose. The devil also has come with purpose. Jesus' purpose is always the opposite of the purposes of the devil! Jesus has come to give you a life that is full of abundance, joy, peace and prosperity. This life that Jesus came to give you is to make you like Him. The devil just plainly wants to "take you out". Why? The devil himself, was once one of the highest creations in heaven. His name was Lucifer. Lucifer said in his heart according to *Isaiah 14:14 "I will ascend above the tops of the clouds; I will make myself like the Most High."* Lucifer wanted to be just like God. He wanted to have all power, and all authority in heaven and in earth. Now that Jesus has come, and has paid the price for us on the cross, He has made a way for us to become like Him. To be changed and transformed into the image of Christ. Jesus came to earth and became human, so that you and I could become like Him. To become Christ-like. To become a new creation. We have been given the right to become children or offspring of God. From the beginning God created us humans in His image.

From the beginning God created mankind to rule and reign and be in His image. The devil hates this! He wanted the position for himself! The devil hates you, and hates me. His purpose is to try to destroy you, because you are made in God's image. It is as simple as that! To be made in the likeness of God is a powerful and beautiful thing. It is hard to even wrap our minds around being made in God's image, especially if we do not know Him as our personal Lord and Savior. If we really think about being made in His image, we have to come to an understanding of the characteristics of our Heavenly Father. Our Heavenly Father: God is all powerful, is all knowing, and is all authority. When God speaks, things happen!

When God spoke, "let there be light", light was then created. God is a person who never has a bad day, who never gets sick, who never gets depressed. God is an eternal person, who is full of peace, love, joy and wisdom. This is the image we are made in! We are wonderfully made because we are made by Him and in His image.

> *Then God said, "Let us make mankind in our image, in our likeness so that they may rule over the fish in the sea, the birds in the sky, over the livestock and all the creatures that move along the ground."*
> *Genesis 1:26 NIV*

It is very interesting to see the first lie told in the Garden of Eden. Let's look at this in Genesis chapter 3:

> ***Vs. 1 Now the serpent was more cunning than any beast of the field which the Lord God had made. And he said to the woman, "Has God indeed said, 'You shall not eat of every tree of***

the garden'?"

Vs. 2 And the woman said to the serpent, "We may eat the fruit of the trees of the garden;

Vs. 3 "but of the fruit of the tree which is in the midst of the garden, God has said, 'You shall not eat it, nor shall you touch it, lest you die.' "

Vs. 4-5 Then the serpent said to the woman, "You will not surely die. "For God knows that in the day you eat of it your eyes will be opened, and you <u>will be like God</u>, knowing good and evil."

The first thing to notice in verse one is that the serpent was more cunning or subtle. The serpent at that time was a beautiful creature that had legs and walked, and was very wise. We can be sure that the serpents in the Garden of Eden are much different today after God cursed the serpent! Satan chose a beautiful and wise animal to manifest himself through. He didn't just show up in a form of satan himself. He wouldn't show up in his manifest demonic form. If he had shown up in his demonic form instead of a "cover up" I'm sure Eve would have told him to "hit the road, Jack!" This is important to note, because our enemy always uses disguises. He doesn't just "announce" himself. If he did, it would sure make things a lot easier in life for all of us!

So what is the big lie that the devil told? If you notice in verses 4-5 of Genesis chapter 3 that his response to Eve in the eating of the fruit of the tree of life was:

*"For God knows that in the day you eat of it your eyes will be opened, and you **will be like God,** knowing good and evil."* This is the very first lie told in history that we know of! He takes The

Truth, and twists it. He states truth in that "you will be like God", but what he did was get Eve to think that she is NOT made in the image of God! Eve was ALREADY made in the image of God because in Genesis in Chapter 1:27 the Word of God says, "*God made mankind in His image*"! The devil successfully got her to believe a lie that she wasn't made in God's image.

The devil is still doing the same thing today! He is still telling people that they are not made in God's image. That they are not "wonderfully made by God." He got Adam and Eve to destroy themselves by sinning or being disobedient to God. It was the open door to sin and death.

The devil doesn't have anything new to throw at us! He still tries to use the same lie. He goes after the image of God because in that image lies the source of God and the power of Almighty God IN YOU. When you lose sight of the image of God, you lose sight of who you are in Christ Jesus and who He has made you to be. It is then the devil goes after the image because he is afraid of it, which makes him afraid of you!

The image of God was everything that the devil wanted to get his hands on when he had residency in "Heaven", but he lost that place. God instead gave His image to YOU and me, and chose to redeem us through His Son, Jesus, so we can become just like Him.

On top of all that, when Jesus came to earth, He not only gave us authority on earth, but gave us all authority in heaven too. He gave us the keys to the Kingdom that whatever we bind on earth is bound in heaven, and whatever you loose on earth is loosed in heaven. What does this verse really mean? Let me help you here… it means whatever <u>YOU ALLOW</u> on earth is allowed in heaven, whatever YOU <u>DIS-ALLOW</u> on earth is dis-allowed in heaven! Think about that for a moment. This is incredible! I love how the NLT Translation puts this verse:

> *"And I will give you the keys of the Kingdom of Heaven. Whatever you forbid on earth will be forbidden in heaven, and whatever you permit on earth will be permitted in heaven." Mt. 16:19 NLT*

God through His Son Jesus has given us more authority than any devil has! We have been given what the devil wanted, what the devil went after and lost. He is one mad dude.

Whatever we bind on earth is bound in heaven. This means we can dis-allow a devil from moving, and that devil will be bound. We can loose a person on earth from a devil, and that person will be free from that demon.   Not only do we have the keys to the Kingdom of God, but the Word of God also says:

> *"...and raised us up together, and made us sit together in the heavenly places in Christ Jesus."*
> *Ephesians 2:6 NKJV*

Through what Jesus did for us on the cross, and His rising up from the grave, He caused you and me to be raised with Him in heavenly places! Jesus is seated at the right hand of the Father, and He has by His grace seated us with Him! Every battle we fight against the devil, if we will understand where we are seated, we will fight that battle from heaven, from the place of victory. We can be on earth and fight our battles from heaven!

When we bind a devil here on earth, we are doing it from a heavenly place, where the devil wanted to be! He wanted the place that Jesus gave us. Is it no wonder the devil wants to kill you? The very thing he wanted, God gave to us!

Let's look at the account in Luke where the 72 disciples returned

> *Vs. 17 The seventy-two returned with joy and said, "Lord even the demons submit to us in your name."*

Firstly notice the disciples recognized that devils exist! They didn't come back and say demons are a figure of our imagination. They came back and acknowledge that demons are real.

Secondly, because of the name of Jesus, not because of any other name… not because of Mohammed's name, not because of Buddha's name… ONLY the name of Jesus will cast devils out! Let's get that straight folks!

Thirdly, you do not have to obey a devil! The devils have to obey you, and do what YOU tell them to do! You have to begin to look at hopelessness, depression, and suicidal thoughts as "devils". When you do, you will realize these things are not you and you can speak to them to leave, and they will have to obey you.

Let's look at Jesus' response to the disciples: *(NKJV)*

> *Vs. 18-19 – He replied, "I saw satan fall like lightning from heaven. I have given you authority to trample on snakes and scorpions and to overcome all the power of the enemy, nothing by any means shall harm you."*

Now, why did Jesus say, he saw "Satan" fall like lightning from heaven when the scriptures in Isaiah 14:12 says, "How you are fallen from heaven, O Lucifer, son of the morning!" Why didn't Jesus say, I saw Lucifer fall as lightning? Jesus wanted you to know that Lucifer no longer has a name. Why? What is the big deal about a name? A name carries authority and power in it. If one of your good friends that you have known for years walks into your home and tells you to "sit up straight" while you are kicking back watching a movie and relaxing, you would probably do nothing. But if the president of the United States walks in and commands you to "sit up", I bet you would sit right up instantly! Now this is an extreme example, but you get my point. A name carries in it authority. *(For more in-depth teaching on authority get my book "A Strong Tower")*

The word of God says that Jesus' name is the name above all other names. That God has exalted Jesus and given him all power and authority, which Jesus turned around and gave us when He said: I have given you authority to trample… Jesus wanted you to know that with His finished work on the cross that He has stripped Lucifer of his name! Jesus whooped the devil so bad that now he doesn't even have a name! The devil no longer has authority. His name is NOT Satan. Satan is just a term that means "adversary" or your "enemy". Satan is not a name, it's a word to describe who we are talking about. That's it.

The good news is, Jesus defeated your enemy! However even though your enemy has been defeated, you still have an enemy. He is sly and his purpose is to get away with illegal acts to kill you, destroy you and steal from you. Our job as born again believers is to enforce our authority Jesus has given us. The demonic realm is nothing to be afraid of, but instead something to be aware of. It would be much easier if a devil just manifested in the flesh or in the natural where you can see him! If we could know it is him attacking us with our natural eyes we would just say, "away with you demon!" but he comes in sly ways in his invisible form, so we must learn how to recognize him.

In our next chapter we will learn how devils operate, so we can identify if they are working in our lives and enforce our authority over him by the Word of God.

CHAPTER SIX
INVISIBLE WAR

*"For though we walk in the flesh,
we do not war according to the flesh.*

*For the weapons of our warfare are not carnal but mighty
in God for pulling down strongholds, casting down
arguments and <u>every high thing</u> that exalts itself against
the knowledge of God, bringing <u>every thought</u> into
captivity to the obedience of Christ, And being in readiness
to revenge all disobedience, when your obedience is
fulfilled. "*

2 Corinthians 10:3-6 NKJV

Whether you like it or not, you are in a war. If there was no war, why would the Bible be telling us that we have weapons of warfare? The war is over your body, soul and spirit. According to the above Bible verse the war zone is in your mind, or your thought life*...*

> *"Casting down arguments and every high thing that
> exalts itself against the knowledge of God, bringing every
> thought into captivity into the obedience of Christ."*

Your thought life is where the rubber meets the road. If you check where your thoughts are now, and rewind your thoughts back six months, you will see that your thoughts have led you where you are today. Your thoughts will take you places in life. Have you ever been in a conversation with someone, and as you are talking to them, you notice they are not listening anymore? Then you proceed to ask them, "Where are you?" You ask them that because in their mind they have gone somewhere else besides your conversation!

We see in the above scripture that thoughts become strongholds in our lives, good or bad. We have learned in earlier chapters that we should "*give NO place to the devil*." The devil gets a stronghold in our lives through our thought process. The more we allow thoughts into our minds that do not line up with the Word of God (which is Gods will), the more strength he gets. This is your invisible enemy! The more you allow your thoughts to line up to the word of God, the greater strength you have in God. *This is your invisible war.*

YOUR THOUGHTS TAKE YOU PLACES

I had found myself in a place of being under the power of a suicide devil because of the thoughts I was allowing into my mind. I had allowed him to lie to me. I didn't know those thoughts were not my thoughts. They were thoughts coming from an outside spiritual entity. For years I had thoughts of failure. That I am a failure and I am no good at anything. I had thoughts that I was ugly and unattractive. I had thoughts that I was stupid, and not smart. I had thoughts of unworthiness, and that I am not lovable. I had thoughts that no one liked me… These types of thoughts took me places. They took me to a place of sadness and depression, but it didn't stop there, those thoughts eventually took me to a place of medicating the depression with alcohol and drugs, to the point of addiction. After years of this, I found myself in a *place* of suicide.

Some people's thoughts have taken them all the way to the mental institution. Medicating your thoughts, medicating your mind, medicating your feelings will not solve anything, nor defeat a suicide devil.

YOUR THOUGHT LIFE IS THE BATTLE GROUND

Your thought life is the battle ground of the invisible war you are in. We are not talking about "positive thinking" – get that out of you head now. Positive thinking and mental ascent will never achieve what God has for you. The secular medical community would tell you that your thoughts are brain activity. That is not the truth. You thoughts reside in your soul, where you mind, will and emotions are.

Your mind is not your brain. Your brain is a muscle physical organ that tells your body what to do and your mind or thought are behind that muscle instructing it how to behave. We are talking about the very fiber of the spiritual realm where thoughts reside. We are talking about your thoughts in the realm of faith, and the promises of God. When you truly believe Gods word (His will) about your life, then when a thought comes that tries to challenge Gods will for your life, you will reject it. The devil will put thoughts in your mind that are NOT your thoughts. This is why the Bible says to take our thoughts "captive", and casting them down, or cast them off you. You must reject those thoughts that do not line up with what the Word of God says about you. If those thoughts don't line up with, "*you are wondrously made by God and that you are Gods masterpiece*" then you know it is not you! Every time you take a thought captive and cast it down, that doesn't line with Gods plan for your life, you just cast out a devil out of your life!

BREAKING DOWN THE BARRIER

The verse below also connects thoughts with "high thing". ***"Casting down arguments and every <u>high thing</u> that exalts itself against the knowledge of God"*** A high thing by definition is: *an elevated structure that causes a barrier.* If you allow *(remember whatever we allow on earth is allowed in heaven, whatever we dis-allow on earth is dis-allowed in heaven)* thoughts that are not from God into your mind on an ongoing basis, then eventually they form a stronghold in your life. They formulate a barrier. This is exactly what your enemy wants to do. A barrier is always designed to keep you out of something or limit you. The devil wants to build a barrier in your thought life between you and God. He wants to put a barrier in your mind that will keep you out of the goodness of God. He wants to put a barrier in between, "you are more than a conqueror in Christ Jesus" so that you cannot operate in "conqueror mode". He wants to put a barrier in between you and ***"For whatever is born of God overcomes the world. And this is the victory that has overcome the world—our faith." 1st John 5:4 NKJV*** He wants to put a barrier in between you and **"…who hath blessed us with all spiritual blessings in heavenly places in Christ". Ephesian 1:3 NKJV** He wants to put a barrier in between you and, ***"by His stripes you were healed." 1 Peter 2:24*** He wants to put a barrier in between you and ***"Don't forget all His benefits of forgiving you of ALL your iniquities and healing you of ALL your diseases."*** He wants to put a barrier in between you and ***"He renews your youth as the eagle." Psalms 103***

If the devil can get you to believe his thoughts are your thoughts, then he has successfully put a barrier in between you and God. God loves you, but God won't force Himself on you. God will not force His word or His ways on you. God is a gentleman God will never leave you nor forsake you. We see Christians all the time commit suicide, did God leave them? No! They instead took on the devils thoughts to the point that there was a stronghold in their mindset, to the point that they gave their will over to the enemy, the devil. It is up to you to cast every lie down. The bible doesn't say, God will cast down every thought for you. The Bible doesn't say that God will take captive every thought for you. The Bible tells us **WE NEED TO DO IT**. When you cast those lying thoughts down, <u>that are NOT your thoughts</u>, then you cast that barrier down that keeps you from the promises of God.

FIERY DARTS

Thoughts that do not line up with the word of God is what the Bible calls, "fiery darts".

"...above all, taking the shield of faith with which you will be able to quench all the fiery darts of the wicked one."
Ephesians 6:16 NKJV

The Bible says, above ALL, in other words, the next few words are very important so pay attention! Above <u>ALL else</u>, be sure you keep the faith in the Word of God over your life, as it is your faith in His Word that will put out those lying thoughts of the devil. Every time you reject or PUT OUT a thought of your mind that doesn't line up to Gods word you PUT IN Gods word. When you PUT IN Gods word into your mind on a daily basis you will find that PUTTING OUT the thoughts that are not your thoughts, but the devils, will be easier and easier to cast them down. The Bible is very clear about our minds, and our minds being connected to the Word of God.

And do not be conformed to this world, but be transformed <u>by the renewing of your mind,</u> that you may prove what is that good and acceptable and <u>perfect will</u> of God. Romans 12:2 NKJV

I love the way the NLT version puts this verse:

"… but let God transform you into a <u>new person by changing the way you think</u>. Then you will learn to know <u>God's will</u> for you, which is good and pleasing and perfect." Romans 12:2 NLT

We have to allow God to change our thinking! Getting saved by His grace is a great miracle and instantaneous! But Jesus doesn't want to leave us where we just got saved, He wants us to grow up into all spiritual things in Him. This takes a daily renewing of your mind to choose life, by choosing His Word as the last thought, as the last word on the subject.

We simply have to change the way we think, and line up our thoughts by faith to His Word, and believe His word. Then when a lying thought comes, that doesn't line up to the Word of God, we know that thought is not of us, and it is our invisible enemy trying to get us to "go places" where we do not wish to go.

ONLY ONE WAY

There is only one way to God and that is through the door of Jesus. Also, there is only one way to change your thinking, and that is by the hearing of the Word of God. Faith comes by hearing, and hearing by the Word of God. It doesn't come by self-help books, it doesn't come by counseling, it doesn't come by the reports of the media, and it comes by the hearing of the Word of God. Jesus is the living Word. You may hear the Word of God in different ways, you may hear the Word of God at your local church, but that usually is not enough! When we hear the Word of God, it feeds our spirit. I don't understand people who just go to church once a week and call it "done" for the week. We don't eat food once a week, we eat every day. What makes us think we can just eat spiritually once a week? We need to hear the Word of God every day! We can put in a teaching CD, or in your personal time with the Lord, reading His Word, He can speak to you. You can get online these days and find all kinds of good teachings from prophets and apostles that will feed you faith, which in return renews your mind and thought life to the Word of God. We can never hear the Word of God too much! The more we meditate on the Word of God, the more that His promises will manifest in our lives. Just like the scripture in Romans says above: *"be transformed __by the renewing of your mind,__ that you may prove what is that good and acceptable and perfect will of God."* When we allow our minds to be renewed, then we prove Gods will in our lives because His will becomes our stronghold, not the devil. His will or His decision that He has made about us becomes the stronghold in our life. When we allow Gods word to be our thoughts then we prove healing happens to us, we prove deliverance happens to us, we prove peace and joy happens to us, we prove abundance and prosperity happens to us, because these are all the will of God. When we believe that "My God shall supply all my need", and meditate on it, think on it, then when the lie of lack comes knocking at your door, you can slam the door shut, and say to it, "no!" – When I have Christ I have everything! The Bible is very clear on what we should be meditating on in our thought life.

> *Finally, brethren, whatsoever things are true, whatsoever things are honest, whatsoever things are just, whatsoever things are pure,*

> *whatsoever things are lovely, whatsoever things are of good report; if there be any virtue, and if there be any praise, <u>think on these things.</u> Philippians 4:8 KJV*

The Bible is clear we are to think about things that are godly and of a good report. That we are not to renew our mind to the world's way of thinking because that will only get us the worlds results. God's ways of thinking will get us Gods results. I don't know about you, but I'll take Gods results any day of the week! God has no limits. God has no barriers. When we get in line with Gods ways, and His word, we step into the world of God without limits.

YOU ARE THE BY PRODUCT OF YOUR THOUGHTS

Have you ever heard, you are what you eat? It is the same thing with your thought life. What you think is what you become.

"For as he thinks in his heart, so is he." Proverbs 23:7a

Not only do our thoughts take us places, but we become what we think!

What? Seriously? Yes! What you meditate on is what you will become. If a person thinks and believe the Word of God has healed them, then they will be healed. If a person goes around always thinking they are a sinner, then you are going to see a person who sins a lot. If a person is always thinking they are sick, you will see a sick person.

It was in 2002, the Lord called me to move out of Alaska and down to Pensacola, Florida to go to bible school to be trained in ministry. This is not just any ordinary bible school, but a bible school that is for every believer who wants to walk in victory in every area of their life. Learning how to cooperate with the Word and Spirit of God to see heaven manifest in our lives and others as we minister to them. I wanted a deeper relationship with Jesus, and I desperately wanted to see the power of the Holy Spirit of God manifest in our ministry. I wanted to see people healed of cancer, healed of broken bones, healed of diseases, and I wanted to see people set free from devils. So I went to International Miracle Institute. It was not easy to leave Alaska at the time, as I lived in Girdwood, with the most majestic view of the mountains you have ever seen! Every morning was like waking up to a movie!

A few weeks after arriving in Pensacola, Florida, I became ill. Oh, I was so ill! It was like my whole body weighed 1000 pounds, my head ached so bad I would get dizzy, and glands had swollen up ten times what they should have been, my bones hurt, everything hurt, and on top of that was nauseated with spats of vomiting. I couldn't keep food down. At first I thought, ah 24 hour flu, just grin and bear it, it will be over soon. A week goes by, and I'm still the same, two weeks go by, I am no better, three weeks go by and I'm worse than I was the first week! I'm now sneaking into miracle school late to slip in the back row, because I don't want anyone to see that I'm sick! How can you go to miracle bible school and be sick?

Finally after several weeks of this, I started going to the doctor. The doctors would take test after test and come back and say, "We don't know what's wrong with you, the tests are not showing anything". Weeks would go by again, and I would go back to the doctor and they would run more tests, and would again say, "We do not know what's wrong with you, the tests aren't showing anything." I was so ill, it was a major chore to do laundry! At this time in my life I am a single woman, living by myself. Being ill like this and single can be very scary. I'm too sick to work, so I don't know how rent is going to be paid, I am too ill to cook for myself, I have no strength left in my body. I have no one to take care of me or help me. Fear began to set in at this point. I kept going back to the doctor. They would run more tests…for seven months they ran tests and could not find anything wrong with me! I kept saying to them, "I'm sick! I'm sick!" In my mind, in my thoughts, I thought I was sick. All I could do at this point was lay on the couch at home and I would listen the CDs of the International Miracle Institute with Drs. Christian & Robin Harfouche's teaching. I would listen to their teachings of the Word of God for hours on end. I did this day after day…only having enough energy to push the play button on the CD player. One day, I went back to the doctor, with tears in my eyes and said, "Doctor, I'm sick, please help me." "Give me something that will make me better!" The doctor looked at me and said, "The next thing we need to test for is cancer." "Cancer!" I said. You never saw a girl run out of the doctor's office so fast. I didn't know a whole lot at that time in the Word and Spirit, but I knew enough to not let anyone speak a curse of "Cancer" over me! There was literally a cloud of dust behind me as I left that doctors office that day!

When I got home from the doctors that day, I resumed my usual position on the couch, where I had been for seven months sick. I put in my International Miracle Institute CDs and let the word of God just go into my ears. After another week of this, something happened. One day as I was listening to those teachings, the Word of God hit my spirit, with the words *"by His stripes you were healed."* and I THOUGHT all of sudden, wait a minute! The Word of God says that Jesus paid the price on the cross for my physical healing! Wait just a minute, back the popsicle truck up! All of a sudden the thought came to me… I AM NOT SICK!!! When this thought hit my spirit, I shot up off the couch, all by myself, I let out a shout out loud, "I AM NOT SICK"!!!! Boom! That was it! I walked right out of that sickness. To this day I have no idea what I had, but I know it was by allowing God's word to change my thoughts to line up to God's will for my life. ***What I thought was what I became.*** When I thought I was sick, I was sick! When I changed my mind that I was healed by Jesus' finished work on the cross I was healed! I choose to walk in divine health. There were times symptoms try to hit my body, but instead of receiving those symptoms in my thought life, I choose to meditate my thoughts on "I am healed, by His stripes."

In the realm of the suicide spirit, what happens is that devil will put on a person thoughts and feelings of hopelessness, despair, depression, sadness, unworthiness. As a person meditates on these thoughts long enough they give place to this devil to BECOME in their lives. Show me a hopeless person, and I'll show you a person who has not been meditating on the Word of God, but instead on their circumstances. Show me a depressed person, and I'll show you a person whose thoughts are nowhere near the living word of God and His promises. We were created to be a people who are walking in victory, joy, peace and love, authority and power. We were created to rule and reign from the beginning. Our bodies, minds and souls were not created to carry grief, sickness, despair, hopelessness, that is why Jesus took those on Himself on the cross, so we do not have to. These things will have a dramatic effect on us if we allow them to continue. Jesus said for us to cast our cares upon Him, because He cares for you, and He cares for me. We tend to think the word "care" means to pat somebody on the back and say "everything is going to be ok." That is not what this verse means. Jesus is not going to pat you on the back and send you on your way with no help! When the Word says that Jesus cares for us, it is like a "care taker". Cast your care upon Him, so that He can **take care of you**! Jesus took on every bit of sin on His body, soul and spirit to the point that He became sin for us, and that sin was crucified on the cross so that we don't have to carry any sin, any burdens, nor any devil!

We are a byproduct of our thoughts!!!! How important is it to meditate on God's word? Very important! If by me changing my thoughts to the will of God set me free from disease, surely if we change our thoughts, renew our mind to the Word of God of who we are in Christ, that we are wonderfully made in His image, and focus on what Jesus has MADE us already we can cast off any devil that is messing with our thought life. We can cast off that spirit of suicide before it gets to be a stronghold in our life. It is when thoughts become a stronghold in our life that we need deliverance. Jesus has paid the price for our body, soul and spirit, as He died on the cross with His body, soul and spirit. It is all paid for in full! All we have to do is yield our thinking to His Word and His ways, and walk right out of those demonic realms of thinking. He has even given us the keys to His kingdom so we can unlock the door that has bound us and trapped us in our thought life. Just walk right out of it, shut the door behind you and do not look back!

We again see this principle of "*as a man thinketh in his heart so is he*" in Psalms 1:2

But his delight is in the law of the Lord,
And in His law he meditates day and night.

He shall be like a tree
Planted by the rivers of water,
That brings forth its fruit in its season,
Whose leaf also shall not wither;
And whatever he does shall prosper. (NKJV)

You see in Psalms that as we meditate on the Word of the Lord day and night, not ceasing, we become! He shall be! When you mediate on the things of the Lord you begin to change and transform your thinking, which causes you to become from the inside out. You become like a well-watered tree planted by the river. A tree by the river is not worried and does not stress about anything. It is just enjoying the sunshine, and soaking up the provision of the river. The tree is not worried about bearing fruit or worried about losing its leaves. Instead that tree is enjoying the life God gave it, and its purpose for bearing fruit happens without striving or effort. This is what happens when you let the Word of God become alive to you by meditating on it. You come to a place when the storms of life come and you recognize those storms are real, and you also recognize that God is bigger than any storm! You recognize that your roots go down deep and there is no wind that can shake you out of your place in God. You come to the place where you know you are fulfilling Gods purpose day by day. We have been given the right to BECOME the children of God! (John 1:12)

Below is a great verse to meditate on! Meditate on the "becoming"...

"For He made Him who knew no sin to be sin for us, that we might BECOME the righteousness of God in Him.
2 Corinthians 5:21 NKJV

CHAPTER SEVEN
TURNED OVER TO THE TORTURERS

Let's take a look at this parable in the Bible that Jesus shared with His disciples that is found in Matthew 18:21-35

> *Then Peter came to Him and said, "Lord, how often shall my brother sin against me, and I forgive him? Up to seven times?"*
>
> *Jesus said to him, "I do not say to you, up to seven times, but up to seventy times seven. "Therefore the kingdom of heaven is like a certain king who wanted to settle accounts with his servants.*
>
> *"And when he had begun to settle accounts, one was brought to him who owed him ten thousand talents.*
> *"But as he was not able to pay, his master commanded that he be sold, with his wife and children and all that he had, and that payment be made.*
>
> *"The servant therefore fell down before him, saying, 'Master, have patience with me, and I will pay you all.'*

"Then the master of that servant was moved with compassion, released him, and forgave him the debt.

"But that servant went out and found one of his fellow servants who owed him a hundred denarii; and he laid hands on him and took him by the throat, saying, 'Pay me what you owe!'
"So his fellow servant fell down at his feet and begged him, saying, 'Have patience with me, and I will pay you all.' And he would not, but went and threw him into prison till he should pay the debt.

"So when his fellow servants saw what had been done, they were very grieved, and came and told their master all that had been done.

"Then his master, after he had called him, said to him, 'You wicked servant! I forgave you all that debt because you begged me. 'Should you not also have had compassion on your fellow servant, just as I had pity on you?'

"And his master was angry, and delivered him to the torturers until he should pay all that was due to him. "So My heavenly Father also will do to you if each of you, from his heart, does not forgive his brother his trespasses."

Another sly trap the enemy loves to use to ensnare us, is unforgiveness. He tries to get us offended with one another to the point that we hold a grudge or are hurt.   If our brother or sister offends us or sins against us, it's to our advantage to forgive them quickly. Even when we know we are in the right, and you didn't do anything wrong, we must forgive unless we be turned over to the torturers.

As you read at the beginning of this book in Chapter One the two things that ensnared me into a place of suicide was lying thoughts from the devil and un-forgiveness towards a ministry colleague that badly wounded me. When I had not forgiven that person, the thoughts that I battled kept coming more and more rapidly. These were thoughts of anger, thoughts of hurt, thoughts of betrayal of things that were done to me. I believed I was right and they were in the wrong, but I didn't want to give up forgiveness to them. I wanted to hold on to my hurt. I wanted to hold on to my anger, because I was "rightfully angry". What happened next is my thoughts became so incredibly crazy, I had no control over them! Thoughts of suicide, thoughts of hurting myself and others were constantly racing through my mind 24/7. I mean it! Twenty-four hours a day my mind was doing non-stop thoughts of suicide AND on top of it, I would have visions in my mind of killing myself with a gun. I was having visions and thoughts tormenting me every day, all day. I was literally being tormented in my thought life! If you have this in your life today, evaluate if you have forgiven everyone, no matter if you were in the right or not. Just forgive!   Once I forgave that ministry, I was instantly set free of that suicide devil that was torturing me. Once you forgive, that devil will have to leave you alone because the door is shut to him.

It might be dangerous for some people to forgive someone in person, depending on what the circumstance was with their situation. You don't always have to verbally say to the person that hurt you, that you "forgive them". Actually, most of the time people use that as an excuse to really say, "You hurt me, but I'm going to forgive you anyway." And it is not heartfelt. This is not forgiveness. If you remember in Chapter One of my testimony, I didn't say to that person who wounded me so badly, "I forgive you." I reached out to them and said, "Please forgive me for anything I did to hurt you." Which in the natural is totally crazy after what was done to me. I realized I was in bondage until I released forgiveness and that's how the Lord led me to do it. Honestly, even though it was the other party who had hurt, me, I was still in the wrong for holding un-forgiveness. When we hold un-forgiveness towards someone that is a direct dis-obedience to Gods word and He cannot bless you, as un-forgiveness is sin. If you are unable to forgive, then you need to ask the Lord to help you in this area, and He will!

All you need to do, is when you pray the prayer at the end of this book to really forgive in your heart those that have offended or wounded you. The Lord will give you the ability to forgive!

CHAPTER EIGHT
PUT THE DEVIL IN HIS PLACE

We have learned in earlier chapters that we should give "no place to the devil". Well, how about putting the devil in his place? Sometimes you hear people say, "I sure put them in their place!" In other words "I shut them up!" It's time to shut the devil up and put him in his place!

Although the devil is defeated by what Jesus did on the cross, he is hoping and betting that you do not believe that. If he can get you to believe he has more power than you, then he can override your will. Your will is where you make your decisions and the devil wants your decision making power to use you for his purposes and kill you.

If we fight the devil on our own, we will get no results. If we fight the devil the way Jesus did, we will get Jesus' results. If we do it the way Jesus did, we will put the devil in his place! The devils place is a place where he cannot penetrate into your life, where he cannot steal from you, nor can he destroy you.

The Word of God says in James 4:7:

> *"Therefore submit to God. Resist the devil and he will flee from you." James 4:7 NKJV*

Notice the first thing you must do is "submit" to God. Submit simply means to "obey". When you put obedience to God and mix it with resisting the devil you have a recipe for freedom! Let's be honest, your way of doing things has gotten you where you are today. Think about it for a minute. To submit to God means to obey Him, which means you need to put off your ways, and your way of thinking and put on His ways and His ways of thinking. The Bible says that our thoughts are not His thoughts and that we must put on the new man or put on the mind of Christ. In order to do this we must simply do what the Bible says to do in fighting the devil.

The way Jesus fought the devil can be found in Matthew chapter 4 where Jesus was led up by the Spirit into the wilderness to be tempted by the devil. He had been fasting forty days, and then He hungered. Let's take a closer look at this account:

> *Matthew 4:3-11*
>
> *Vs 3 Now when the tempter came to Him, he said, "If You are the Son of God, command that these stones become bread."*
>
> *Vs 4 But He answered and said, "<u>IT IS WRITTEN</u>, Man shall not live by bread alone, but by every word that proceeds from the mouth of God."*
>
> *Vs 5 Then the devil took Him up into the holy city, set Him on the pinnacle of the temple,*
>
> *Vs 6 and said to Him, "If You are the Son of God, throw yourself down. "For it is written: He shall give His angels charge over you, and in their hands they shall bear you up, lest you dash your foot against a stone.'"*

Vs 7 Jesus said to him, "IT IS WRITTEN AGAIN, You shall not tempt the Lord your God.'"

Vs 8 Again the devil took Him up on an exceedingly high mountain, and showed Him all the kingdoms of the world and their glory.

Vs 9 and he said to Him, "All these things I will give You if You will fall down and worship me."

Vs 10 Then Jesus said to him, "Away with you, Satan! For IT IS WRITTEN, 'You shall worship the Lord your God and Him only you shall serve.'"

Vs. 11 THEN THE DEVIL LEFT HIM, AND, BEHOLD, ANGELS CAME AND MINISTERED TO HIM.

Notice every time the devil tried to tempt Jesus that His response was the Word of God, **IT IS WRITTEN**. Jesus didn't wave a magic wand and point it at the devil and then he disappeared. No! Jesus Himself, as a man on earth, responded to the devil each time with the Word of God.

When the devil comes to you, and tries to make you feel depressed, or tries to make you feel unworthy, or tries to make you feel there is "no reason for living", you must respond to him and say, **IT IS WRITTEN** and read the Bible back to him! The devil has no power over the Word of God. The Word of God will always put the devil in his place! It is important to note that the devil does COME to you. John 10:10 says, *"When the thief comes, he comes to kill, steal and destroy."* You can be assured the devil will come! When the devil does come to you with those lying emotions, feeling and thoughts, then quote the Word of God, (without doubting) back at him. Say, "Devil! IT IS WRITTEN, according the 1st John 4:4, 'Greater is He that is in me than he that is in the world.'" "Therefore, devil, God is bigger than anything you can throw at me!"

To use the Word of God against the devil you MUST KNOW **and** BELIEVE the Word of God. It's not just enough to know the word and quote the word, you must also BELIEVE the Word of God. IT IS WRITTEN is your answer for the rest of your life in anything the devil throws at you! By knowing and believing the Word of God and speaking it back to the devil is submitting yourself to God. The devil cannot stand the Word of God!

There is a reason it says in Ephesian 6:17 –

> *"Take up the helmet of salvation, and the SWORD OF THE SPIRIT, WHICH IS THE WORD OF GOD." Ephesians 6:17 (NKJV)*

The Word of God is part of your offensive and defensive weapons in God! It will cut off the devil in your life. The devil is defenseless against it, but you MUST BELIEVE the Word of God. The Word of God will put the devil in "his place" every time! You cannot just "quote" it to the devil and not believe it. Even the devil "quotes" the Word of God. The Word of God says that he who doubts is double-minded and will NOT receive anything from the Lord. (James 1:6) Starve your doubt and unbelief, as they are not your friends, but instead they are your enemies, as they will keep you out of the goodness of God for your life. The Word of God needs to come out from your innermost being. We are to live and abide in Him, or live and abide in the Word of God with all our hearts, mind and soul.

Notice that the devil didn't just try to tempt Jesus once. Why do we think that once the devil leaves us that he won't come back? The devil will always come back to try to "pull one over on you". That is just how he operates. You need to know that you will have great success in using the Word of God at your enemy, the devil, but he will return again, and again.

The Bible says Jesus would cast out spirits with a word. We have that same power. Whether it is a devil pestering us, or another person. I was recently ministering in one of the villages of Alaska. We had powerful gatherings, the anointing was strong in the place. People were getting healed right in their seats. Broken bones were being instantly healed, people were jumping out of their seats healed. We lined everyone up at the end of the gathering to lay hands for impartation for everyone who wanted it. I noticed one of the Eskimo men who was helping to assist people who were being overcome by the presence of the Holy Spirit and who wasn't "clean" or had some devils on him.

I thought the pastor of the group had assigned him to help catch, so I just figured he had been approved. I didn't know that the guy who had devils on him, just jumped up there by himself to help. Well as the anointing is hitting each person I lay hands on, it's also hitting this large Eskimo man while he is catching. The anointing is beginning to drive those devils to the surface, and he is sweating like there is no tomorrow.

After we went through and laid hands on everyone, this man was the last person to minister to. He is drenched now in the anointing. I laid my hands on him and I said with a command, "GO!" and all of a sudden the man fell out under the power of the Holy Spirit and was growling and choking and manifesting devils. I jumped on him and began casting out devils one after the other, commanding them to leave this man. Devil after devil would leave. I would command him to look at me, so I could see if we had gotten all the devils out. After going through several layers of devils he began to manifest even greater to the point I had to put the man in a head lock and ask my husband to pin him down.

Now I have this large Eskimo man in a head lock, working the works of Christ to see him set free. He is trying to get away from me or Christ in me. I finally grab his head and get him to a place to look at me. I command the devil to "look at me! As the man opens his eyes, it's me on top of him, but Christ in me looking at the devil face to face. All of a sudden the love of God fills me as I'm looking at this man, but also looking at the devil that has a hold of him, and as the love of God fills me looking right at this devil in the eye, I say, *"It is written, perfect love casts out all fear."* As soon as I said that the last devil, the spirit of fear immediately left this man and he was set free and began to praise God. He jumped up off the floor and raised his hands to heaven and began to give God the glory for his deliverance. The word of God, is God. God is love. When we use the living Word of God the devil cannot stand it, and he cannot stay! The power of love of God will cast out any devil!

After I received my deliverance from the spirit of suicide, the devil tried to come back a few times after. The devil's plan was to try to get me to fall into his ways again, but I was all the wiser after my deliverance. I could recognize it was the devil, and therefore when he came to try to tempt me to take my life again, I told him OUT LOUD, "Devil, you have no place in me, I am a new creation, and I belong to God, leave me!" The devil tried to come back a few times. Each time I just used the sword of the Word of God, I stayed submitted to God, I resisted the devil, and then he left me. Now he knows he cannot tempt me in this area, and doesn't even try anymore. He realizes in this area of my life, suicide has been totally defeated and I will not tolerate him in my life. What really helped me to get, know, and believe God's word was the International Miracle Institute. Any person who gets on this bible school will be equipped to handle by the Word of God anything the devil might throw at them. The International Miracle Institute will bring to life the Word of God IN YOU and will establish you in God's Kingdom. You can get information about this bible school at the back of the book.

I find it very interesting that in Verse 6 above that the devil even temps Jesus to "jump". The devil tempts Jesus to take His own life by "jumping". Even the Lord was tempted by the devil to take His own life, but Jesus didn't consider it for one moment. Jesus didn't give it any thought, but instead, battled it with the Word of God.

Jesus, in the wilderness did James 4:7. Although He was God just as much as a man, Jesus was functioning on earth in His humanness when He was in the wilderness. In Matthew chapter 4, Jesus submitted Himself to God, and He resisted the devil and the devil had to leave! Jesus showed us plainly how to fight the devil. **IT IS WRITTEN, we must be doers of the Word of God, not just hearers. (James 1:22)**

CHAPTER NINE
GUARD YOUR HEART

"Guard your heart above all else,
for it determines the course of your life.
Proverbs 4:23 New Living Translation

Hurt. We have all been there. There is not one person on this planet that has not been hurt by another person. Some people guard their hearts by being cold-hearted and not having a relationship with the body of Christ. This is not what this verse is implying. A closed out heart will not guard your heart, but instead will just make you hard hearted, and that is not what the Lord desires for us.

The verse above is clearly telling us that our heart will determine our future. This is pretty important to pay attention to! If you heart is hurt all the time, then it will take you on a course of pain and destruction, but a heart that is joyful and peaceful will take you in a completely different direction. Guarding your heart is guarding your future!

> *"Whoever has no rule over his own spirit is like a city broken down, without walls." Proverbs 25:28 NKJV*

Walls. Some people have walls you can't get past. This is not the kind of walls the Lord wants you to have. Your spirit is to have walls, but the right kind of walls. If you guard your heart by trusting in God's word and keeping a watch on your thought life, those are walls that the devil cannot penetrate. If you get slack in your thought life, and what is coming out your mouth, then your spiritual walls are broken down and you are a wide open target for the enemy to move in.

The second deliverance from suicide I went through, was due to un-forgiveness that we identified as an open door for the devil. If I had kept my heart guarded, I would have never fell into that trap of un-forgiveness where I was turned over to the torturers.

Our heart in this verse means: mind, thinking, reflection, memory. What you are guarding is what comes into your mind and thinking. Thoughts are how the enemy tries to "take a place" in our lives. Guarding your thoughts is guarding your heart. Guarding your mind is guarding your heart.

SAY OUT LOUD:

"WHEN I GUARD WHAT COMES INTO MY MIND, I GUARD MY HEART."

"WHEN I GUARD MY THOGHT LIFE, AND CAST DOWN THOUGHTS THAT DO NOT LINE UP WITH THE WORD OF GOD, I GUARD MY HEART."

"WHEN I GUARD WHAT COMES INTO MY EARS, I GUARD MY HEART."

"WHEN I GUARD WHAT COMES INTO MY EYES, I GUARD MY HEART."

The hurt will direct and determine the path of our lives we allow it. Hurt never leads to the path that God has for us. Instead, it leads us to a life of bondage and is certainly an open door for the devil to work in our lives. All of us have the opportunity to respond to hurtful words. It is not other people's responsibility to guard our hearts. No one is responsible for our heart except us. We cannot blame our heart condition on what others have done to us. Well, what about abuse, Maria? I have been abused physically and sexually. I don't doubt that one is hurt due to physical and sexual abuse. I have been through both domestic violence as well as sexually violated. Although what was done to me and you was wrong and certainly was not Gods will, we are still the ones responsible for pursuing God to allow HIM to heal us. God is faithful, and He will never let you down. He is willing to heal you and He will do it. Look at what *1 Thessalonians says in 5:23-24 NKJV:*

> *"Now may the God of peace Himself sanctify you completely; and may your __whole spirit, soul, and body__ be preserved blameless at the coming of our Lord Jesus Christ. He who calls you is faithful, __who also will do it."__*

God is more than willing to heal us body, soul and spirit! The Bible says, "He will do it"! What more could we ask for? He is not going to do a partial job either, but the Word of God says, "Completely". He will completely heal you!

It is not about blame anyways, it is about receiving His love, His healing, His forgiveness in your heart that will set you free of past wounds and hurts. The key to that is forgiveness and then allowing the Holy Spirit to come minister to your heart. You do that through times of worship unto *the Lord, times of prayer, times of being in the Lords presence. It is in His presence where we find healing.* Everyone is at different levels in their healing process. Although complete healing is available it takes some longer than others to receive healing, as we cannot earn it. We can only receive it.

On a side note: God doesn't call us to be a doormat either. If you are in a violent situation, you have every right to remove yourself from that situation, as it is not Gods will for you to be harmed. If your life is being threatened, then you need to get out! You still have to practice forgiveness towards that person, but that doesn't mean you need to "live" with the violence.

Just like the woman with the issue of blood in Luke 8. Can you imagine the emotional and mental torture this woman must have gone through to have an issue of blood for twelve years and no doctor could help her? How she was most likely labeled "unclean" for twelve years! And can you imagine the procedures the doctors must have put her through physically, as doctors in those days certainly didn't have the technology we have today! It was when this woman got into the presence of Jesus that she was able to receive a miracle. When Jesus wasn't around, there was no miracle. When she got close to Him, and reached out with her HEART and touched Him, He responded back with the power of love flowing out of Him. He responded to the disciples… "Who touched me?" There were people all around thronging Jesus and yet none of them received a miracle. No one else reached out to Jesus with their heart!!! Only one woman reached out to Him with her heart. When you reach out to Jesus with your heart, He hears you every time and responds appropriately. I believe this woman not only received a physical miracle, but received healing in her soul from probably all kinds of abuse of what people said about her, and maybe even what she thought about herself.

It's important to note with this woman, that when she did reach out with her heart, the bible says, she said in her heart, "If I may only touch the hem of His garment I WILL be made whole." (Matthew 9:21) Notice she said, "I WILL". Your will plays a key factor in your healing and deliverance. She made a decision that when she touched the Masters garment that she would be, not maybe, not some day, but that she WOULD BE HEALED, and she was! When she lined up her will, her decision making faculty with Gods will, then there was an explosion of healing power from heaven in her life!

Guarding also what comes into your ears and eyes is also guarding your heart. When people say stupid things to you, you do not have to allow those things into your mind, into your spirit. You can choose to love those people, despite the stupid things they are saying. This does not mean that we reject people, but it does mean that when they are operating in "stupid" mode that we make a choice to not be offended and not "take it to heart". Instead, do what the bible says, *"A gentle answer turns away anger..."* **Proverbs 15:1** HCSB Translation. When a person attacks you with words, try responding with a kind word to them, and watch them change their tune. Cover them with love and watch and see what God will do in that situation. I think we are all working on this! I know I am working on practicing this more and more in my life.

We have to learn to guard our hearts from the devil, not from people. Our war is not against flesh and blood the Bible says, but against principalities and powers. The devil will at many times try to use people to get to your heart, this is why your heart has to be guarded. But you have to identify the spirit that's operating behind a person when they try to hurt you and be quick to forgive.

> *"Behold, I give you the authority to trample on*
> *serpents and scorpions, and over all the power*

of the enemy, and nothing shall by any means hurt you. Luke 10:19 NKJV

NEVER HURT AGAIN?

What?   Never hurt again?   Our minds have a hard time comprehending this, but the bible says *"… and nothing shall by any means hurt you*." I did not make that up, it's just Bible. How can that be? What is this verse implying? Whatever we can find in the Bible, in the Word of God we can HAVE it! If we can find it in the Word of God, then it means we have access to it. It is possible for us to never be hurt again, but it will take our will being involved in agreeing with the Word of God and applying it.

Let's take a closer look at this verse. Serpents in this verse means "a sly, cunning one", and "scorpion" means "to pierce". Jesus has said that we have all authority over the power of the devil. He is sly, he is cunning and he comes to hurt us, and many times uses people to do it through! Jesus continues on to say that NOTHING shall by any means hurt you. This is wild! The word "hurt" in this verse means, "socially or physically". This means that we do not have to be hurt physically or socially again. This means that we never again have to be hurt by other people.

Even the Apostle Paul understood this in Acts Chapter 28. During his travels on his way to the Roman Empire for trial, he finds himself shipwrecked on the island of Malta. On that island while hanging out with the islanders around the fire, a very poisonous snake jumped out of the wood and locked its fangs in him. All the islanders thought for sure he was going to die. Obviously the islanders knew the power of the poison of the snake, or they would not have been so shocked when Paul lived.

What did the Apostle Paul do when he got bit and the poison was loosed into his flesh? He shook his hand, and shook that snake off into the fire!

> **"But he shook off the creature into the fire and suffered no harm." Acts 28:5 NKJV**

God never promised us we wouldn't get bit! But God does promise we do not have to be harmed when we do get bitten! The Word of God promises us trials and tribulations, but the Word of God also promises that if we trust in Him, if we live in Him, if we abide in Jesus, that we will have victory and success over it all!

How we respond when we get bit is the key. Our will is involved. Our will is our decision making faculty. If we decide today, if we decide now that when we get bit, that it will not harm us, then when something like that happens we can just shake it into the fire! This is something that all of us have to walk out for the rest of our lives on this earth. It comes down to this, hurt is a choice. We can choose if we are going to be hurt by a circumstance or not.

Forgiveness also is a choice of the will. We can choose to forgive or not forgive. This is the power that has been given to us. We are stewards of this power and how we use it. I encourage each one of you to choose Wisely. The Word of God also encourages you to choose wisely… in Deuteronomy 30:19 I have set before you life and death, blessing and cursing; therefore choose life, that both you and your descendants may live."

We all know that forgiveness sometimes can be hard to do. We need the power of the Holy Spirit to help us. Jesus said, "*without Me you can do nothing.*" (John 15:5) In other words, with Him, we can do everything! We need to ask for His help in this area. Jesus also said that He would send us a "Helper" the Holy Spirit.

> **"But I tell you the truth, it is to your advantage that I go away; for if I do not go away, the Helper will not come to you; but if I go, I will send Him to you." John 16:7**

Jesus didn't leave us without help! If you need help with forgiveness just pray this prayer right now from your heart:

Father, I come to you today for help by your precious Holy Spirit. I need to forgive, and I am unable to do so in my own power and ability. I need your ability Lord. I can do nothing without you Jesus. I ask you to help me forgive this person, and heal my heart today, in the Name of Jesus. Amen.

Forgiveness is something that we all walk out the rest of our lives. So we might as well practice it now and get used to it!

When we choose to forgive quickly, and choose to not be offended, and stay in His love, we have guarded our hearts and we will live a life that is full of freedom, love, joy and peace in Christ Jesus.   A life of victory.

CHAPTER TEN
CALLED TO GREATNESS

I am so thankful to God in what He has brought me through. There have been others who didn't make it and chose to end their life early. If I hadn't been saved and delivered by the Lord Jesus Christ, I would have never had the opportunity to step into His plan and purposes for my life.

Since the healing and deliverance in my own life, God has restored me in so many ways. He has restored my relationship with my family, and other relationships that had been damaged in the past. He has restored a fantastic loving husband who loves to travel with me when I preach in the villages of Alaska.

The Lord Jesus Christ not only took away the spirit of suicide off my life, but he delivered me from a spirit of shame. Those that have been sexually abused know what I'm talking about. The Lord will also deliver you today from the spirit of shame and by the power of the Holy Spirit the power of shame will be broken off you life.

Instead of your shame you will receive a double portion, and instead of disgrace you will rejoice in your inheritance. And so you will inherit a double portion in your land, and everlasting joy will be yours. Isaiah 61:7

He has taught me to walk by faith, and not by sight, not by hurt, not by wounded-ness, but instead to walk by His Spirit. When you walk by faith, you step into His greatness into what He can do <u>for you and through you</u>. By walking in faith, I have had the privilege to see God use me in funneling hundreds of thousands of dollar's worth of goods to needy families, and medical supplies to foreign counties as well as preach the Gospel of Christ from Africa to Alaska. God has used me to put new shoes on hundreds of children's feet and help parents who need assistance with diapers for their children.

God has blessed me and allowed me to minister His healing to many people. I have had the privilege to see the Lord not only heal hearts and spirits, but see Him do great and mighty works in peoples bodies. I have watched people come in with braces, crutches, walkers and then walk out of our miracle meetings without them. I have watched people come in with tumors and growths and watch them dissolve by the power of the Holy Spirit. I have watched people be set free of addiction, depression, suicide, and even cancer. None of this has been by my own doing and efforts. All of the goodness and restoration in my life has been by His Spirit. The word of God says, "*It is not by mans' might, not by man's power, but by My Spirit says, the Lord.*" *(Zechariah 4:6)*

There is nothing more satisfying then stepping into the high call of Gods greatness for your life!

If God can heal a person like me from sexual abuse, depression, suicide and addiction, He can do it for you! If God can take a person like me, who thought she was a failure at everything, and unlovable, hated herself and restored her back to a life that is full of Gods abundance and use her in a mighty way, He can do that for you!

You may not know it right now, but you are called to greatness! God's masterpieces are not called to a life of defeat, but a life full of love and success.

> *"Before I formed you in the womb I knew you, before you were born I set you apart..."*
> *Jeremiah 1:5*

> *"You didn't choose me, remember; I chose*

> **you, and put you in the world to bear fruit, fruit**
> **that won't spoil. As fruit bearers, whatever you**
> **ask the Father in relation to me, he gives you."**
> **John 15:16 Message Translation**

God knew you before you were even in your mother's womb. God's greatest work, **you**, have a destiny and purpose in Him. God has chosen you for this very hour that you live in. He has not chosen for you to end your life pre-maturely. It is no accident you have picked up this book, God led you to this book. How do I know? I know because He instructed me to write this book, and every word has been written under the inspiration of His Holy Spirit for **YOU.** You were not an accident, you have been designed and chosen by God! He has chosen you to read this book, and He has chosen you to a God kind of life of good works in Him.

> **For we are God's masterpiece. He has created**
> **us anew in Christ Jesus, so we can do the**
> **GOOD THINGS HE HAS PLANNED FOR US**
> **LONG AGO. Ephesians 2:20 NLT**

Not only are you God's best piece of work, God has good things prepared for your life right now! These things for your life have been planned long ago. Remember the devil has a plan for your life, and God has a plan for your life. Which one will you choose today with your will?

He has a place for you in Him for eternity if you will receive Him and allow Him to be your Savior and Lord, and allow Him to work in you.

There is no better words I can leave you with today, than this prophetic word that was given by the Holy Spirit through my father in the faith, *Apostle Christian Harfouche*, receive these words from the Lord Jesus for your life today:

> *There is a place prepared for you.*
> *for those chosen of God,*
> *There is a realm available to you.*

you can rise and enter on in,
Even now the glory of the Lord belongs to you,
    and He will show you how,
There is a realm where the yoke will break
    and the things of old will become no more.
There is a place for you reserved
    a higher place for a higher call
And anyone who has received His grace
    can enter in and win the race
There is a place that belongs to you

There is a place of glory, this is true,
    a supernatural realm, a heavenly sphere,
That place is not way up there, no, no it's here, it's here,
    so come on and enter in,
    and wave goodbye to every failure and the state of sin,
Come on in and watch your past instantly diminish,
    it will not last,
Come on in, and allow the balm to heal your heart
    and sing a song,
Come on in to this realm
    and allow Christ the Anointed One …

Oh let the wind of God blow in your sail,
    and surely, surely you will prevail.
Oh don't look on up and say He is beyond the sky
    and don't wonder or ask the question why,
No He is not up there that you have to bring Him down,
    and He is not below, He's not even around, He is within,
He is upon, He is here even now,
    to answer your every need, your every desire,
So come on in says the Spirit of the Lord
    and drink freely with one accord,
And the weight of the burden will fall by the wayside,
    and the things that used to bind, they will no longer be
    able to hide,

And you will say I went over there to the river you see,
    and I gained from the Lord victorious liberty,
I went in depressed, but I went out with joy,
    I have to share it, I have to tell about Gods mighty ploy
How He spoiled the devil, hell and the grave
    how victory and blessing to The Church He gave,

I must tell it I must preach, I have to prophesy
   I have to teach,

There is a place, a place that belongs to you…

GOD HAS A PLACE FOR YOU, IT IS A PLACE OF GREATNESS, AND DESTINY. DON'T GIVE UP, BUT INSTEAD GIVE YOUR LIFE OVER TO JESUS TODAY BY PRAYING THE PRAYER OF SALVATION AND DELIVERANCE IN THE NEXT CHAPTER

PRAYER OF DELIVERANCE

> *"And it shall come to pass in that day, that his burden*
> *shall be taken away from off thy shoulder, and his*
> *yoke from off thy neck, and the yoke shall be destroyed*
> *because of the anointing.*
> *Isaiah 10:27 KJV*

What is a yoke? A yoke is a bondage that controls a person. Yokes were used to guide oxen, to control them where they wanted them to go. That is what the devil does when he puts a yoke on a person. He gains that control and guides you where you do not want to go. The anointing destroys this yoke! The anointing destroys this bondage!

Jesus is the only answer to a spirit of suicide, depression or addiction. The bible says:

> **I am the door. If anyone enters by Me, he will**
> **be saved, and will go in and out and find**
> **pasture. John 10:9 NKJ**

Jesus is the only door to God. There is no other way to God but through the door of Christ and what He did for us on the cross.

If there is a doorway, there is a porch. The bible refers to devils as "dogs" in several places. It's time to leave the dog on the porch and go through the door of Christ.

> *"Behold, here comes the Lamb of God that <u>TAKES AWAY</u> the sin of the world."*
> *John 1:29*

If you are desperate for change in your life, if you are tired of being harassed by outside demonic forces, and you are ready for deliverance, then I would like to lead you in a prayer to pray out loud and mean it in your heart. It is not the prayer that delivers you, but your connection with the anointing. The anointing is "Christ in action". Jesus is alive, He is no longer on that cross. He is alive! The Bible says that He died to pay the price for all sin, which includes devils and rose from the dead for our redemption, in other words to belong to God again.

He has already done the work. He has already taken away the sin of the world. He has already made His decision about YOU! He has decided from before you were born that you are free in Him not bound by devils. Now His anointing will destroy that thing that has gotten on you as an outside force trying to overcome your mind and will. You should not pray this prayer until you are ready to receive from God and believe that He will work in your life. You should not be in a hurry, but pray this prayer when you have time to sit in His presence and let the His Holy Spirit minister to you by His anointing that will destroy every yoke.

PRAYER OF DELIVERANCE:

Pray out loud:

Father, I come to you in the name of Jesus, and I recognize my sin, and ask you to forgive me of ALL my sin. Lord you know all my sin, please forgive me for each and every one, and wash me clean with your Word. I acknowledge, Father God that you sent your son Jesus on the cross to pay for my sin, to pay for my punishment that I could not pay. I recognize I do not deserve anything of my own works, but I receive what Jesus has done for me today in the area of salvation, deliverance, healing and prosperity. I recognize today, that Jesus is alive and is risen from the dead, seated at your right hand.

Father, forgive me for holding un-forgiveness towards those who have hurt me. I forgive right now, ALL who have hurt me in the past, and ask you to release me from the torturers. I forgive them Lord. I hold no grudge against them, I release them to You, Father.

Father I ask you to forgive me for those I have hurt in life.

I ask you Lord, to forgive me for any occult activities I have practiced in my life, and any occult practices that my forefathers have done. I repent of all occult activity in my life and/or my family's life. I repent and ask forgiveness for having other gods in my life and not trusting you. I ask you Lord to forgive me of allowing the devil into my thought life and for allowing the devil to put on lying symptoms of depressions, despair, hopelessness, unworthiness. I ask you Lord to forgive me for turning to drugs and alcohol instead of to You. I ask you to forgive me of addiction.

Before you Father God, I renounce every spirit attached to the occult now, it has no place in my life. I renounce the spirit of suicide, depression, anxiety and addiction.

Devil, it is written that I have all authority and all power over you as it says in Luke 10:19. So I speak to you spirit of suicide and I say, Spirit of suicide, depression, anxiety, and spirit of fear you cannot live in my life anymore, I command you to leave me. I do not want you in my life, and I loose you from me according to Matthew 18:18 that whatever I allow on earth is allowed in heaven, and whatever I disallow on earth is dis-allowed in heaven. I disallow you, spirit of suicide! GO! (Command it to go!)

Devil, it is written that you shall worship the Lord God only as according to Luke 4:8. So I speak to you spirit of addiction and I say, *"Spirit of addiction, you cannot live in my life anymore, I command you to leave me. I do not want you in my life, and I loose you from me as according to Matthew 18:18 that whatever I allow on earth is allowed in heaven, and whatever I disallow on earth is dis-allowed in heaven. I disallow you, spirit of addiction! GO!"* (Command it to go!)

Father, I receive your precious Holy Spirit now to destroy this yoke according to your word in Isaiah 10:27, and I receive the infilling of your Holy Spirit of power and anointing that destroys every yoke in my life. Fill me now, Lord.

Now raise your hands to heaven in thanksgiving out loud, and allow the Holy Spirit to come and minister to you. Thank Him that you are free! Worship Him. Let His presence wash over you. Let peace take your mind and allow the joy of the Lord to fill you. Take time with Him every day.

Email us, and let us know you have been set free!

Contact Dr. Maria immediately, she wants to hear from you! You can contact her through her website at: www.MariaKrinock.com

NEXT STEP:

To stay free, and have the Lord establish you, it is important to find a SPIRIT FILLED local church in your area, and to be well rooted in the love and Word of God.

I personally believe once a week on Sunday not enough. We eat regular food more than once a week, why is it that we think eating spiritually once a week is enough? I recommend you get a hold of as many spirit filled resources as possible to feed your spirit. There are many good ministries out there these days.

I personally recommend: *Year 1 of International Miracle Institute* for your training in the Word of God. It's a bible school for every believer who wants to walk in the power of God. I have personally gone through this training and can recommend it to anyone who desires to be well fed in the Word and Spirit of God. It changed my life, and it will change yours too!

More information on International Miracle Institute:

www.imilive.org or email: imi@globalrevival.com

A WORD TO THOSE WHO HAVE LOST LOVED ONES TO SUICIDE

I cannot imagine what it must be like to lose a family member or friend to the spirit of suicide, but my heart goes out to each and every person who has ever lost a close loved one. The only words I could even give you, would be to hold onto Jesus and let Him minister to your heart, and allow Him to heal you, no matter how long it takes. He loves you, and it was never His plan for that to happen in your family.

This is a very sad thing, and again my heart goes out to each and every one of you. I would like to also encourage you that you did nothing wrong, it was not your fault, and it was not Gods fault. If there is anyone to blame or put at fault, it is the devil.

Jesus said, "The thief (the devil) comes to kill, steal and destroy,
but I have come that they may have life,
and life more abundantly." John 10:10

We must rise up and educate people of the spiritual forces that lie at the door awaiting to devour Gods people. We also must educate people of the power of the Holy Spirit that will destroy every ounce of bondage that the devil may throw at the people of God.

For those of you who know what it is like to lose a loved one to suicide, I encourage you to pray about partnering with us to get this book out into the villages of Alaska and beyond. Together we can make a difference in saving lives.   Let's not let another one be taken by this evil spirit!

You can learn more about partnering with us at our website:
www.mariakrinock.com

OUR ALASKA JOURNEY SO FAR...

All glory and honor to Jesus Christ for every miracle, healing, salvation, and deliverance in these photos. Without Him I can do nothing, but with Him ALL things are possible!

ANCHORAGE, ALASKA

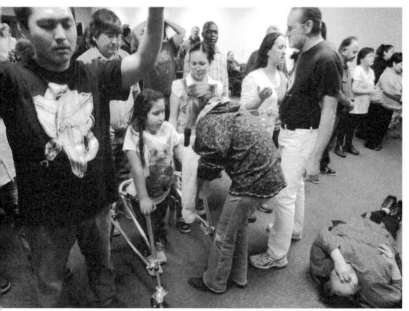

BARROW, ALASKA

NECK INJURY HEALED, NO MORE PAIN!

LOVE THESE GUYS AND GALS!

BETHEL ALASKA

**FEEL LIKE SHOOTIN' SOME DEVILS!
BETHEL, ALASKA**

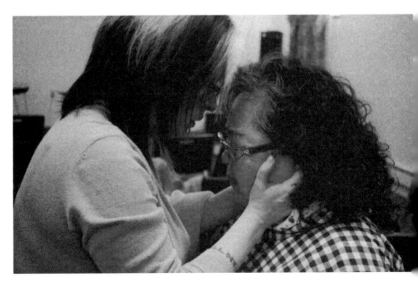

BUCKLAND, ALASKA

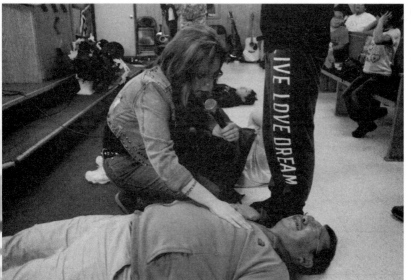

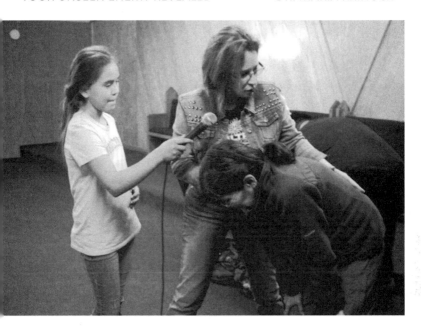

CHEVAK, ALASKA

GAMBELL, ALASKA
ST. LAWRENCE ISLAND

POLLY TESTIFYING HOW JESUS HEALED
HER CRIPPLED ARM

FRIENDS OF GAMBELL, ALASKA

HOMER, ALASKA

**WORSHIP LEADER TESTIFYING HIS ARTHRITIS
OF 10 YEARS IS COMPLETLY HEALED &
NO LONGER NEEDS PAIN MEDS BEFORE HE PLAYS GUITAR.**

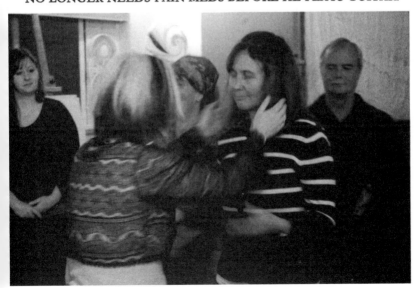

KIVALINA, ALASKA

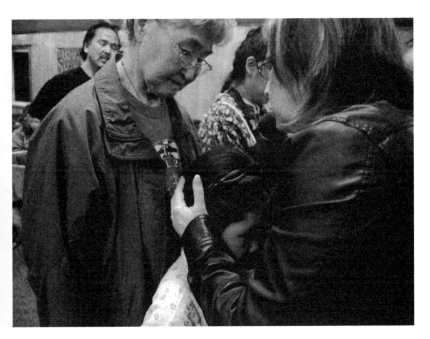

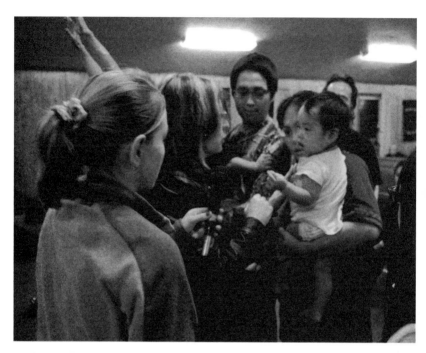

KODIAK, ALASKA
MAN, GETTING COMPLETE MIRALCLE IN
HIS SKELATAL SYSTEM FROM HEAD TO TOE.

ANGIE, TESTIFYING
OF BEING HEALED OF SCOLIOSIS,
AND
BEING FREE OF YEARS OF PAIN

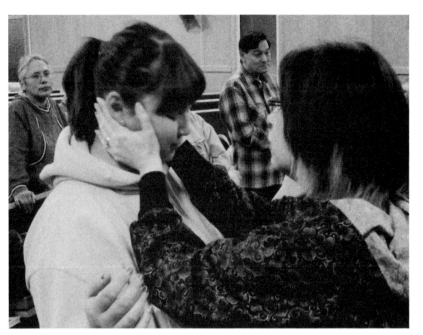

KOTZEBUE, ALASKA

NOATAK, ALASKA

BERNICE, OVERCOME WITH JOY
THAT JESUS HEALED HER BROKEN ANKLE.

OMG! TOO CUTE!!!!

NOME, ALASKA
WOMEN OF FREEDOM
CONFERENCE

NORTH POLE, ALASKA

POINT HOPE, ALASKA

SAVOONGA, ALASKA
ST. LAWRENCE ISLAND

SHUNGNAK, ALASKA

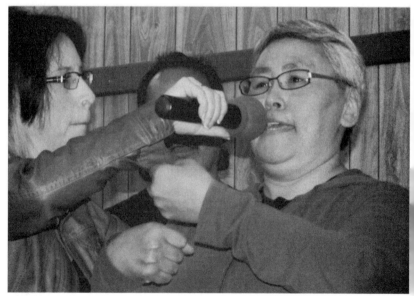

**PASTOR AVIS TESTIFYING OF HER SPINE
BEING HEALED**

SHUNGNAK, AK

PREPARING FOR THE WORD OF GOD
ON CARIBOU HIDE

HIP & BONES BEING TOTALLY HEALED & SEVERE ARTHITUS HEALED

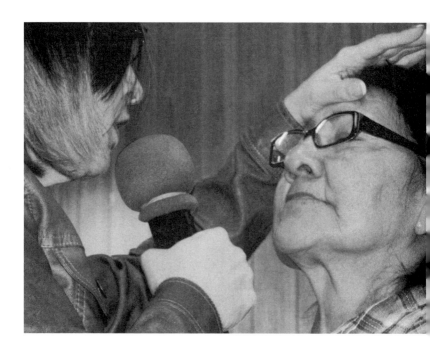

SOLDOTNA, ALASKA

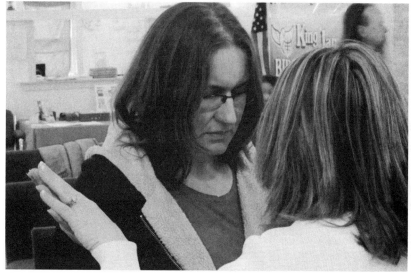

SPECIAL "THANKS"TO THE AMAZING ALASKA HELPS
MINISTRY TEAM!!

*You are so special in our hearts… we couldn't of done the
Lord's work without you!*

ABOUT THE AUTHOR:

Dr. Maria Krinock has invested over 16 years with International Miracle Institute with Drs. Christian & Robin Harfouche. Through International Miracle Institute, Dr. Maria has acquired a Doctorate of Divinity and Doctorate of Ministry.

Flowing strongly in the gift of working of miracles, Maria has a passion to see the body of Christ living in the realm of victory, no matter what opposing circumstance they may be facing. Maria equips the body of Christ with a biblical word of supply that ignites the very heart of people to go to the next level in their walk with Christ.

Maria and her husband have invested thousands of gospel dollars in making sure the anointing reaches the villages of Alaska in demonstration and power of the Holy Spirit. Together they have seen the cripple walk, broken bones instantly healed, tumors dissolve, and terminal disease flee and much more!

In the last hour we live in, Dr. Maria and her husband Conrad are more determined than ever to see the harvest of souls for the Kingdom of God.

To have Dr. Maria Krinock come to your area, email: contact@lifelineoutreach.com or visit her website at: www.MariaKrinock.com

GENERAL INFORMATION

To contact Dr. Maria Krinock for any of the following reasons:

1. To have Dr. Maria come to your area
2. To order *Your Unseen Enemy Revealed* in bulk.
3. To email Dr. Maria your prayer request
4. Share your testimony
5. To give a donation to Dr. Maria's ministry

Please make contact via website :

www.MariaKrinock.com

FRIEND DR. MARIA ON FACEBOOK:
https://www.facebook.com/maria.magruder.krinock

WEBSITES:

WWW.MARIAKRINOCK.COM
WWW.LIFELINEOUTREACH.COM

REACHING EVERY VILLAGE IN ALASKA

OUR GOAL IS TO DEPOSIT THESE BOOKS IN EVERY VILLAGE.

BE A PART AND HELP SPONSOR BOOKS!
www.MariaKrinock.com